TABLE OF CONTENTS

LIST OF FIGURES AND TABLES

Part II

AN EXAMINATION OF NOISE ABATEMENT POLICIES IN SIX COUNTRIES

LIST OF INSETS

FIGHTING
NOISE
IN THE 1990s

ORGANISATION FOR ECONOMIC CO-OPERATION AND DEVELOPMENT

Pursuant to Article 1 of the Convention signed in Paris on 14th December 1960, and which came into force on 30th September 1961, the Organisation for Economic Co-operation and Development (OECD) shall promote policies designed:

- to achieve the highest sustainable economic growth and employment and a rising standard of living in Member countries, while maintaining financial stability, and thus to contribute to the development of the world economy;
- to contribute to sound economic expansion in Member as well as non-member countries in the process of economic development; and
- to contribute to the expansion of world trade on a multilateral, non-discriminatory basis in accordance with international obligations.

The original Member countries of the OECD are Austria, Belgium, Canada, Denmark, France, Germany, Greece, Iceland, Ireland, Italy, Luxembourg, the Netherlands, Norway, Portugal, Spain, Sweden, Switzerland, Turkey, the United Kingdom and the United States. The following countries became Members subsequently through accession at the dates indicated hereafter: Japan (28th April 1964), Finland (28th January 1969), Australia (7th June 1971) and New Zealand (29th May 1973). The Commission of the European Communities takes part in the work of the OECD (Article 13 of the OECD Convention). Yugoslavia takes part in some of the work of the OECD (agreement of 28th October 1961).

Publié en français sous le titre :

LUTTER CONTRE LE BRUIT
DANS LES ANNÉES 90

© photo Réunion des musées nationaux
Ceremonial anthropomorphological mask
Photo Mario Carrieri

In 1987 the OECD Environment Committee launched a project on noise abatement policies in Member countries.

The aim of the project was to collect information on the effective implementation of such policies in selected countries. For this purpose case studies were carried out in six countries: Australia, France, Germany, Japan, the Netherlands and Switzerland.

The case studies helped with the analysis of problems arising in the OECD countries: motor vehicle noise, aircraft noise, railway noise, industrial noise and neighbourhood noise. In addition, as part of the same project, the OECD made a special study of the use made of incentives of all kinds to encourage the manufacture and use of silent products, equipment and vehicles.

The report that follows assesses the relative effectiveness of the various elements of noise abatement policies. It describes what has been done and what remains to be done in the six countries covered by the case studies. Although the assessment and conclusions reached concern the six countries in particular, many of the findings and proposals made in the report could equally well apply to other OECD countries.

Part I of this report gives a critical assessment of the implementation of noise abatement policies, particularly as regards the use of economic and non–economic incentives and the extent to which regulations are actually enforced.

The assessment is based on the six case studies undertaken by independent experts, and consisting of a description, an analysis and an assessment of policies applied in the country concerned.

Part II contains a comparative description of policies pursued in the six above countries and supplements the assessment which has deliberately been kept brief. This dual approach — evaluation and description — seems to be the best way of helping countries achieve a better understanding of what is being done and of what could be done. The assessment which follows also reflects the conclusions of the OECD Conference of 1980 and the OECD Council Recommendation on Noise Abatement Policies of 20th June 1985.

The drafting of this report has been overseen by National Experts on noise from Member countries, assisted by Messrs Ariel Alexandre and Jean–Philippe Barde from the OECD Secretariat.

Two consultants — Mr Pierre Chapuy (France) and Ms Jill Shankleman (United Kingdom) — contributed to the drafting of this report.

Also available

THE STATE OF THE ENVIRONMENT (1991)
(97 91 01 1) ISBN 92–64–13442–5   FF180   £22.00   US$38.00   DM70

CONTROL STRATEGIES FOR PHOTOCHEMICAL OXIDANTS ACROSS EUROPE (1990)
(97 90 01 1) ISBN 92–64–13401–8   FF125   £15.00   US$26.00   DM49

OECD ENVIRONMENTAL DATA — COMPENDIUM 1989/DONNÉES OCDE SUR
L'ENVIRONNEMENT — COMPENDIUM 1989 (Bilingual)
(97 89 03 3) ISBN 92–64–03223–1   FF220   £26.50   US$46.50   DM91

ECONOMIC INSTRUMENTS FOR ENVIRONMENTAL PROTECTION (1989)
(97 89 04 1) ISBN 92–64–13251–1   FF110   £13.50   US$23.50   DM46

To be published

OECD ENVIRONMENTAL DATA — COMPENDIUM 1991/ DONNÉES OCDE SUR L'EN-
VIRONNEMENT — COMPENDIUM 1991 (Bilingual)

Prices charged at the OECD Bookshop.
The OECD CATALOGUE OF PUBLICATIONS and supplements will be sent free of charge
on request addressed either to OECD Publications Service,
2, rue André–Pascal, 75775 PARIS CEDEX 16,
or to the OECD Distributor in your country

LIST OF FIGURES AND TABLES

7

SUMMARY

Analysis of recent trends regarding both exposure to noise and implementation of noise abatement policies gives no ground for optimism as to the future development of the acoustic environment.

In the light of the figures available (which tend to become increasingly less regular and standardized), it seems that exposure of populations to noise has stabilized or increased so far as "black spots" are concerned; it has, on the other hand, significantly deteriorated in most countries as the "grey" areas have grown larger. "Grey areas" are those where the situation is not exceptionally bad but is far from being satisfactory.

Increasing road and air traffic is the main reason for this, and the outlook seems rather poor, particularly in the light of the rates of growth in numbers of vehicles and mobility observed since 1985. Neighbourhood noise is having a considerable impact on populations but measures taken against this form of nuisance seem inadequate in practically all countries.

Changes in noise sources and their continuous rapid growth over recent years constitute a challenge which, on the whole, noise abatement policies pursued in the majority of OECD countries have not succeeded in meeting; nor, have they met the expectations of the public, for which noise is one of its major concerns in regard to the local environment and the quality of life.

In many countries, the ambitions of the policies pursued are limited by the slender resources allocated to them, by inadequate enforcement of available regulations and, more generally, by the absence of any consistent and co–ordinated strategy among the various public and private actors. Even in those more countries where some more ambitious strategy has been implemented, the results obtained and the programmes pursued do not seem likely to be adequate to deal with future problems.

Thus, at the beginning of the 1990s, considerable efforts remain to be made in the OECD countries to develop and strengthen noise abatement policies, provided, of course, that noise abatement is still seen as forming an integral part of policies to improve the environment, particularly the urban environment.

If further deterioration of the acoustic environment is to be prevented, noise abatement policies should include the following elements:

— Develop a coherent national strategy;
— Co–ordinate this policy between national, regional and local authorities;
— Provide the resources needed for proper enforcement of measures adopted;
— Monitor policy implementation;
— Generalise the use of economic and non–economic incentives;
— Take vigourous steps to change the behaviour of the public and of decision–makers;
— Integrate noise concerns in the development of transport policies and traffic management policies;
— In the longer term, introduce stricter emission limits for the noisiest vehicles and equipment.

Part I

AN ASSESSMENT OF NOISE ABATEMENT POLICIES

Chapter 1

THE STATE OF THE NOISE ENVIRONMENT
AND CURRENT TRENDS

The effectiveness of noise abatement policies will be examined with reference to the current state of the noise environment and ways in which it is changing, by assessing the respective impacts and weights of the four main sources of noise covered by this report:

— Road traffic;
— Air traffic;
— Rail traffic;
— Neighbourhood noise (domestic appliances, gardening equipment, dogs, etc.)[1].

1. SERIOUS SHORTCOMINGS IN OBSERVATION AND MEASUREMENT

Compared to the measurements made and data available for some components of the environment which directly affect man, such as air or water, observation of the noise environment is still highly inadequate. In many OECD countries, measurement of noise levels and of the exposure of populations is far from comprehensive. Measurement is usually undertaken at irregular intervals and coverage is not total. It is striking that most data available to OECD on exposure to noise have not been updated for some five to ten years.

The percentages of national populations exposed to transport noise for the six countries covered by the case studies show a large number of gaps (particularly for aircraft and railway noise) (Table 1). For OECD as a whole, only 15 countries out of 24 have data on exposure to noise, and the figures are often incomplete or out of date, or are estimates based on somewhat simplistic models[2]. As a result, it is difficult to discern the overall trend of exposure of populations to noise nuisance from the main sources (road, air and rail traffic).

Available data show that exposure to noise, which was fairly stable at the beginning of the 1980s, has increased in certain countries (e.g. France, Germany, the Netherlands, Switzerland) due to the rapid growth in traffic (road traffic volume rose about 30 per cent in OECD countries from 1980 to 1989). Exposure to high noise levels have stabilized in some cases and increased in others (Leq above 65 dB(A)); on the other hand, the number of people living in "grey areas" (i.e. exposed to levels between 55 and 65 dB(A)) has significantly increased[3].

13

The tightening of standards (EC limits were lowered by 5 dB(A) for private cars and 6 to 7 dB(A) for lorries between 1972 and 1988) and other steps to reduce noise, such as new infrastructure, noise protection screens along main highways, etc., have offset to some extent the increase in traffic but without producing any real improvement.

Continued urban development — characterised by the spread of residential suburbs and housing in rural areas near towns, a fall in the population of town centres where noise levels are highest, and steps to eliminate "black spots" — has indeed considerably alleviated the worst situations, but has also greatly enlarged the "grey areas" of exposure to noise.

The outlook is not good, assuming that the rapid growth of traffic, particularly road and air traffic, noted over the last two years, is likely to continue in a period of sustained economic development.

The diagnosis of the state of the noise environment and probable trends seems therefore to have changed little in recent years, although there is a risk of more rapid deterioration in the near future. Furthermore, the relative inaccuracy of noise environment data in most OECD countries poses problems, for any reliable analysis should take account of local circumstances and of noise abatement projects worthy being limited elsewhere.

Some review of noise indicators used so far is called for. Today, noise exposure is assessed by measuring a kind of average noise level in front of the façades of buildings (most often using the index Leq over 18 hours and in Japan, the index L50, a noise level which is exceeded 50 per cent of the time). Although this day–time Leq is seen as the most appropriate indicator, this single indicator could be usefully complemented by others, such as night–time or evening–period Leq, as well as indicators for peaks of noise. Only with these additional indicators would the noise situation and nuisance be fully described, reflecting evening and night–time traffic, isolated noise sources in a relatively quiet area, and unpleasant low frequencies from heavy lorries, sport cars or leisure equipment and installations.

Road traffic

In spite of stricter emission limits[4], traffic growth and its extension to new time periods and new areas have tended to make things worse in areas with average noise, i.e. the "grey areas" where noise levels are between 55 and 65 dB(A) (measured in Leq 08.00–22.00 or 06.00–22.00 according to countries).

In France, for example, the urban population (towns with over 5 000 inhabitants) exposed to noise levels between 55 and 65 dB(A) rose from 13 to 14 million between 1975 and 1985. In the Netherlands, during roughly the same period (from 1977 to 1987), surveys show that the percentage of the population claiming moderate disturbance from road traffic increased from 48 to 60 per cent.

In the same period catching–up policies pursued in several countries dealt with some "black spots" over 65 dB(A) or 70 dB(A), but primarily with the worst ones. In France, the urban population exposed to noise in the "black areas" (over 65 dB(A)) between 1975 and 1985 remained constant at 6 million people, while in the Netherlands, people claiming serious noise disturbance due to road traffic remained at 20 per cent between 1977 and 1987. In the absence of regular detailed surveys in most countries it is nevertheless difficult to measure exactly to what extent previously existing "black spots" have or have not been dealt with.

14

Table 1. **Exposure of national population to transport noise**

Six countries studied

Unit: percentage[a,f]

Country	Year	Outside noise level in L_{eq} (dB(A))[b]														
		Road transport noise					Aircraft noise					Railway noise				
		>55	>60	>65	>70	>75	>55	>60	>65	>70	>75	>55	>60	>65	>70	>75
Australia	–	46.0	..	8.0	..	..	..	..	..	..	..	..	..	..	..	..
Japan[c]	1980	80.0	58.0	31.0	10.0	1.0	3.0	..	0.5	0.2	0.1	..	..	..	..	..
France[d]	1985	54.4	33.1	16.6	5.5	0.6	..	1.0	..	..	..	..	..	..	..	..
Germany	1985	45.0	26.7	12.5	5.1	1.1	..	..	1.0	..	0.2	18.0	8.4	2.9	0.8	0.1
Netherlands	1987	54.0	20.0	4.1	1.3	–	36.0	15.0	0.4	0.1	–	6.0	1.5	0.6	0.3	0.1
Switzerland[e]	1985	53.7	26.3	11.7	4.1	0.7	2.0	1.0	0.6	0.7	–	23.4	13.0	5.9	2.5	0.9

a) The percentages are cumulative and not additive (e.g., the percentage of people exposed to over 55 dB(A) includes the figure for people exposed to over 60 dB(A), etc.).
b) Daytime L_{eq} (00.06-22.00) measured in front of the most exposed facades of buildings.
c) OECD estimates.
d) L_{eq} (00.08-20.00); urban areas (over 5 000 inh.); data refer to all facades of buildings.
e) Aircraft: 1980 figures.
f) .. not available
   – nil or neglible.
Source: OECD Environmental Data.

It is also difficult, in view of likely traffic growth and proposed catching–up programmes, to assess to what extent these black spots and others that may appear in the future, along existing or new routes (some countries are planning to build new infrastructure to cope with growing demand), will be dealt with satisfactorily. In some countries, it is clear in view of the funds committed that catching–up programmes are not adequate; in some cases, it is going to take nearly 40 years to eliminate "black spots". Other countries expect to deal with acute noise problems (including "black spots" along highways) in 15 years. There are only two possibilities: either funds allocated for this purpose are going to be generally inadequate, or they will have to be backed up by financial measures to make road users pay part of the necessary expense. This point will be discussed later.

The trend of population exposure to noise will depend on numerous factors, chiefly traffic growth and future urban development, and on the scope of the noise abatement policies implemented. Traffic growth is very closely linked to economic growth.

In the Netherlands, for example, the number of private cars could increase from 4.6 million in 1985 to 7.9 million by the year 2010 and passenger traffic by road could increase by nearly 70 per cent over the same period; the outlook for goods traffic by road seems to be for an even bigger increase, in the absence of deliberate policy to limit or penalise certain forms of transport. In France, growth in the number of private cars could reach 40 to 60 per cent between 1985 and 2010 in accordance with various feasible scenarios; goods traffic by road could increase by 30 to 50 per cent over the same period.

In this context, prospects investigated in various countries show that failing a significant stepping up of noise abatement policies and better enforcement, exposure to noise will on the whole increase even though local improvements may be brought about by deliberate policy measures such as the prohibition of traffic in certain areas, construction of noise screens along main highways and the re–routing of traffic. Furthermore, it is of growing importance, when new noise emission limits are discussed, to analyse the need for limits concerning tyre noise; presently, tyre/road noise often determines the noise level of individual vehicles, at least for free–flowing traffic.

Air traffic

The end of the 1970s and the beginning of the 1980s were marked by a fall in noise levels around nearly all commercial airports. This improvement was due essentially to the increasing use of quieter planes. Stricter noise certification standards have been applied under the auspices of the International Civil Aviation Organisation (ICAO, Annex 16, Chapters 2 and 3). This has been made possible by new engine technologies, since the research leading to the large energy savings achieved by manufacturers has helped to produce jet engines that are also less noisy. Moreover, most OECD countries now do not allow aircraft without noise certificates to land at their airports.

Since 1985, air traffic has increased rapidly, often by as much as 10 per cent per year. This is causing the state of the noise environment to level out or even deteriorate around certain airports and thus offsets the benefits of technological progress and regulations. The probable trend of exposure to aircraft noise is now less hopeful than it was at the beginning of the 1980s, in view of the expected growth of air traffic in the OECD countries.

What is more, in many countries the pressure of building and other signs of economic development on land near airports is making it difficult to keep such areas clear of housing;

hence it is likely that, with time, the numbers of people exposed to high or unacceptable noise levels will increase. How can proper allowance for noise be made in local planning policies for areas near airports? This problem, found to some extent in all the OECD countries, together with increasing traffic, leaves little room for hope of rapid improvement in diminishing noise from air transport.

Small propeller aircraft also create potential noise nuisance and the nuisance value of increasing helicopter traffic as well has become steadily more acute.

Rail traffic

Problems of railway noise vary considerably from one country to another, depending mainly on the size of the rail network, on geography and on density of housing. The percentage of the population exposed is high primarily in Switzerland, where urban areas are limited by the Alps, and to a lesser extent in Germany and the Netherlands and along special routes in Japan. Catching-up programmes are being applied on routes causing the greatest disturbance — in Japan, for example (along the Shinkansen high-speed train route) and in Switzerland.

The general outlook for railway noise and exposure to it is not at all clear. The building of more high-speed rail lines often across frontiers, in Europe, for example, could also make this problem more acute in the future despite the fact that today it is easier to allow for noise in designing and building railways than is the case with roads.

Neighbourhood noise

In most OECD countries neighbourhood noise is seen as a major nuisance, possibly the worst one judging from the results of noise surveys. For example, in the Netherlands, the proportion of the population claiming moderate disturbance by neighbourhood noise rose from 40 to 66 per cent from 1977 to 1987, and the proportion claiming extreme discomfort from 15 to 26 per cent.

Recent trends suggest that the problem of neighourhood noise will remain a primary concern or, at any rate, the nuisance most complained about. As buildings come to be better soundproofed from the outside world, often for reasons connected with thermal insulation, residents can be expected to become more sensitive to noise within dwellings or other buildings, particularly in flats and multi-storey blocks.

Moreover, the situation will probably worsen in the future as sources of neighbourhood noise become more numerous and the power of domestic appliances of all kinds — e.g. kitchen apparatus, hi-fi sets, chain saws, lawn-mowers, leisure products for children and adults — increases. Stricter acoustic requirements have not kept pace with the spread of such devices and manufacturers and distributors do not always comply with them properly. The rising expectations of the public in this area will make the problem worse, as people increasingly seek at home the peace and quiet which may become more and more difficult to find in the outside world, at work and in public places.

Furthermore, to the extent that neighbourhood noise involves personal and social relationships and lifestyles, it will certainly prove to be one of the most difficult problems to resolve in terms of local environmental management.

2. THE OUTLOOK FOR EXPOSURE TO NOISE

The expected increase in numbers of noise sources is likely to lead to deterioration of the noise environment, whilst the increasing awareness and growing expectations of the public will lead to an increase in what is perceived as noise problems in the future, failing strengthened and more strictly applied abatement policies. The deterioration would result primarily from the following factors:

— Increasingly numerous and powerful sources of noise (transport, domestic appliances, etc.) of which increasing use is made (greater mobility and leisure time);
— The wider geographical dispersion of noise sources, owing both to urban development and the construction of new road and rail links, together with greater individual mobility and the spread of leisure activities and tourism to both country and nature areas;
— The spread of noise over time, particularly in the early morning, evenings and weekends;
— Rising public expectations. In the case of the environment, these are known to be closely linked to incomes and education levels, both of which are likely to continue to rise in the OECD countries.

Enforcement of the most recently adopted emission limits will not be enough to reverse current trends and bring about an improvement in a field which most opinion polls show remains a primary public concern. Means have to be sought to improve the state of the noise environment, in the OECD countries, by endeavouring to:

— Strengthen present noise abatement policies and improve their application;
— Support such efforts by a further tightening up of emission standards;
— Closely co-ordinate noise abatement measures and transport planning, particularly by policies designed to reduce mobility or hinder its further development.
— Co-ordinate noise abatement measures with local urban planning.

Chapter 2

REGULATIONS

As in other fields, government measures to reduce noise involve five kinds of function:

— **Planning**, i.e. deciding the future orientation and use of resources, guiding and co–ordinating choices to be made by all those concerned;
— **Regulating**, i.e. defining the "rules of the game";
— **Enforcement** of regulations, i.e. the exercise or delegation of supervisory powers to ensure compliance with laws and regulations, and powers related to the police and the courts;
— **Incentives**, i.e. economic or non–economic measures to persuade all the parties concerned (public or private) but without constraints to act in certain ways;
— **Investment**, i.e. deciding how to allocate public funds (infrastructure, equipment, research, staff, etc.).

These functions are shared among different tiers of government, primarily central and local government, and also federated states or their equivalent (cantons, provinces, Länder) in federal countries.

1.   TWO TYPES OF "PHILOSOPHIES"

Two apparently contradictory approaches or "philosophies" underlie noise abatement policies in the OECD countries:

— In the first, government tackles noise problems only when people complain about them or when conflicts arise, and deals with problems one after the other: action is largely on a blow–by–blow basis, giving priority to resolving the worst problems ("black spots") while neglecting any concerted effort to bring about a general improvement;
— In the second approach, government tackles noise problems from the standpoint of public health and environmental quality objectives.   Such an approach is thus independent of whether or to what extent complaints have been made, and of the types of noise or sources complained of.   The approach is a more global and comprehensive one.   It is also more co–ordinated and consistent.

However, in most of the countries studied, the "blow–by–blow" approach is the one currently used, either deliberately or as a matter of practice.   Only two countries are clearly committed to a global and consistent approach, namely the Netherlands[5] and Switzerland[6] (see Part II).

In reality the two approaches are less contradictory than might appear and sometimes go hand–in–hand. This is the case, for example, in federal countries and in countries where local authorities have considerable autonomy.

The two approaches can of course also be used one after the other: i.e. a "blow–by–blow" policy framework can be replaced by legislation or a proper programme to extend and make noise abatement comprehensive, as has been done in the Netherlands and Switzerland.

In the light of the results of noise abatement efforts so far, it is clear that only a global approach can ensure that the various control measures are coherent and co–ordinated; this was repeatedly emphasized at the OECD's Conference on Noise Abatement Policies in 1980.

2. OBJECTIVES: RARELY EXPLICIT AND QUANTIFIED

In most countries the objectives of noise abatement policies are neither explicit nor quantified at either national or local level. This failing has a number of negative consequences, it:

— Makes it difficult to define a coherent and planned strategy;
— Compromises concerted action by all those involved in noise control (national and local decision–makers, manufacturers and planners, businessmen and consumers);
— Makes it difficult to mobilise and allocate not only financial resources but also the human resources necessary to give effect to policies;
— Does not facilitate the expression of demands for a better environment.

This general absence of clearly defined objectives makes several things difficult or even virtually impossible:

— Evaluation or record of the results of policies;
— Adjustment of policies in the light of their performance and of changing problems and resources (urbanisation, traffic, lifestyles, technologies);
— Monitoring of policy implementation by users, environmental protection associations and noise victims.

The opposite situation is found in two countries. In Switzerland, the clearly proclaimed determination to resolve noise problems within 15 years is supported by a detailed inventory of "black spots" (e.g. along roads and railways) and the provision of funds to deal with them, at least so far as national infrastructure is concerned. Similarly, in the Netherlands, an extremely comprehensive programme sets out detailed objectives to be attained and resources required and is, moreover, regularly updated and assessed.

3. EMISSION STANDARDS: CAN THEY BE MADE STRICTER THAN THE INTERNATIONAL AVERAGE?

Only Switzerland, today, applies motor vehicle noise limits which are practically in line with the OECD recommendations of 1980 (see Part II). But it must be emphasized that little by little other countries are now aligning themselves with the OECD recommendations: Japan, the Nordic countries and gradually the European Community. Switzerland imposes the strictest noise limits in the world for a large number of vehicles and power–driven appliances (cars, light aircraft, motor cycles, lorries, etc.). According to the Swiss authorities this policy is implemented without major problems of either technical feasibility or industrial capacity, provided that the time to be allowed for compliance is announced for enough in advance. In any case the limits have little effect on the range of goods transported and thus do not restrict consumer choice.

Where the necessary technological research and industrial investment have been carried out, the technical advances needed are thus already available today. They could probably be rapidly applied in other countries at little or, in some cases, zero cost.

4. CO–ORDINATION: FREQUENTLY INADEQUATE

In most countries, it seems that too little is done to co–ordinate the action of the various administrative authorities involved in noise abatement. In a number of cases measures are adopted by central government (zoning, dealing with black spots, checks on vehicles, reduction of neighbourhood noise, etc.) but there is no prior co–ordination with agencies responsible for local enforcement; the measures then prove difficult to apply.

In certain countries, for example, the police are held responsible for noise caused by vehicles in service. Where the police are answerable to central rather than local authorities, it becomes difficult to ensure that noise abatement in towns is consistent.

Furthermore, failure to consider consistency and hierarchical relationships among the different types of noise abatement (at source, on transmission, on reception) or among different sources (outside noise, noise in buildings, in schools or at work) runs counter to the optimum use of resources and so to effective national and local action.

In the Netherlands, however, the approach is consistent, hierarchical and co–ordinated. It is based on framework legislation on noise and multi–year noise abatement programmes. Revised each year to take account of changing problems and results obtained, these programmes also provide the resources necessary for implementation, including police and finance.

Elsewhere, however, in the absence of such an approach, it is impossible to tackle the problem of multi–exposure to noise from various sources, i.e. the quality of the acoustic environment in daily life at home, at work and in school.

5. FREQUENT IMBALANCE IN GOVERNMENT ACTION

In most countries, government naturally exercises the five functions listed at the beginning of this section (planning, regulation, enforcement, incentives and investment). In general, however, although the regulating and, to some extent, investment functions have been extensively used in OECD countries, the planning, enforcement and incentives functions are much less to the forefront in noise abatement. Some examples will help illustrate this:

— Vehicle emission limits are enforced at the time of certification and manufacture of a new vehicle. Apart from Australia and Switzerland, few countries successfully test ageing in–service vehicles which can be technically tampered with by individuals, particularly in the case of two–wheeled vehicles; moreover, successful experiments in one town are not always applied throughout the country;

— Standards for the soundproofing of new housing from outside noise now seem to be satisfactory in many countries, but only in very few countries are these standards complied with by all builders and properly enforced by the authorities;

— Noise certification standards for aircraft have significantly reduced noise around airports, but few airports have effective checks on the flight paths of aircraft at take–off; the successful experiment to control aircraft noise at Zurich Airport could usefully be applied generally (see Part II, Inset 7).

More generally, in many countries, the lack of consideration for noise issues at the planning level is particularly damaging when it occurs in the context of general town planning activities, such as local physical development plans, planning of infrastructures and industrial activities, and planning or extension of housing areas. This generally leads to poor prevention of future noise problems. Moreover, the pressure of habitat or economic activities on urban land available for development near important noise sources, such as existing major roads or other infrastructures, is often difficult to control if noise regulations are weakly enforced in urban planning. Planning policies to control urban development in the vicinity of airports, for instance, should be much more effective and applied in due time. What is the point of stricter standards if planning and control of urban development remain lax?

Regulations and programmes, which are not effectively implemented and do not benefit from a political determination to enforce them, merely waste resources without producing the expected results.

6. INTERNATIONAL STANDARDS: ADVANTAGES AND DRAWBACKS

In many areas of noise abatement, international standards are established because of what is at stake economically and because there are international markets for the products concerned. This applies to motor vehicles (United Nations' Economic Commission for Europe — ECE Geneva and European Community — EC Brussels) and commercial aircraft (International Civil Aviation Organisation — ICAO), in particular.

Advantages are several: international standards are naturally of use in a country where political determination is less marked than in others. They enable the country to give effect to policies which, if negotiated at national level, would perhaps have succumbed in the face of opposition from economic or local interests. This international dimension also means that approaches have to be more consistent. It also clarifies and standardizes as between countries the roles of the different parties, whether industrialists or consumers; these standards also help efforts to remove obstacles to trade. Unfortunately, international standards are sometimes defined by reference to this last economic objective rather than with any determination to make real progress towards noise abatement.

Conversely, the international "constraint" expressed in such standards can also have negative effects, e.g. standardization at a level of consensus below what some countries would like to see implemented. This can put an end to any progress both in the short term, by countries which would like to apply stricter standards, and in the long term, since there is no longer any incentive for technical innovation (see also "Environmental Policy and Technical Change", OECD, 1985). The opposite can happen, however, as was recently the case in respect of air pollution by motor vehicles: the level of international standards can be higher than the local consensus level.

However, in some countries, incentive policies and local or selective prohibitions enable international standards to be reinforced. The policies on low–noise vehicles in Germany and the Netherlands provide examples (see Chapters 4 and 5).

Such incentives thus make it possible to give effect to more vigorous policies and to prepare the way for technical developments which will in time facilitate the strengthening of international standards. Stricter policies are thus possible within certain limits. What these limits should be — within the European Community, for example — is a delicate matter.

In view of the time it takes to define new standards and the complex problems involved, it is vital for the OECD countries, or groups of countries (particularly the European Community), rapidly to define rules for those national policies which go beyond the general consensus. This concerns economic and non–economic incentives for the use of low–noise vehicles in particular.

Chapter 3

POLICY IMPLEMENTATION AND LOCAL ACTIONS

1. NOISE: A LOW POLICY PRIORITY

Noise will continue to be a problem, and there is increasing public desire for a better quality local environment and concern that noise sources and places affected will increase in the future.

It is therefore surprising to note a discrepancy in most countries: although opinion polls show that noise often heads the list of concerns about the local environment, it is rarely given priority in environmental policies either at national or local level.

Explanations for this can be sought in the nature of noise nuisance itself:

— There is limited knowledge about exposure to noise, and limited measurement of its effects, compared with other pollution problems;
— The large number of sources of noise and the local character of many noise problems (neighbourhood noise, in particular) which make it difficult to take any coherent action; it may even be felt that action is impossible in some cases;
— Lack of training and awareness on the part of decision–makers in regard to noise problems;
— The absence of major accidents due to noise, whereas many advances in environmental policy have been made following serious accidents: nobody is killed by noise;
— The fact that effects on physical and mental health, although today fairly well understood, are generally not yet seen by the authorities as a source of serious damage;
— The apparently temporary and fleeting nature of noise: unlike pollution, noise does not accumulate over time and its most directly perceivable consequence, discomfort, seems, to most people, to disappear once the noise ceases;
— The fact that some residential districts are fairly well protected so far as noise is concerned, unlike the situation concerning air pollution, for example.

2. MONITORING: OFTEN LIMITED

Monitoring of policy implementation by the authorities is an essential stage of government action: it makes clear, in practice, whether policies have proved effective and reveals the key variables involved.

Nonetheless, considerable difficulty is noted in most countries in "monitoring" implementation of national policies by local authorities, or by states, regions, provinces or cantons in federal countries. Whether for political, institutional or budgetary reasons, the resources and effort given over to monitoring are limited, not to say non–existent. Yet only such detailed observation can make subsequent corrections or adjustment to policies possible in the light of observed results[7] (Figure 1).

Figure 1. **THE ENVIRONMENTAL QUALITY MANAGEMENT CYCLE**

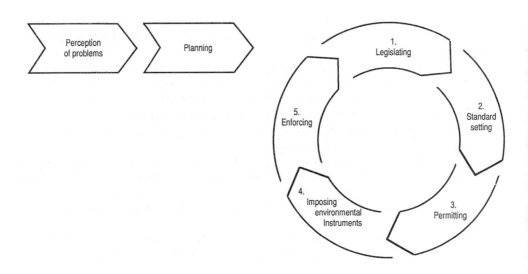

Note : Adapted from the Ministry of housing, Planning and Environment: "Environmental Programme of Netherlands" (January 1985).

Source : "Improving the Enforcement of Environmental Policy", OECD, Paris, 1987.

Even in the Netherlands — where national noise abatement strategy is probably the most exhaustive and the most closely co–ordinated and where monitoring of environmental policy implementation is seen as a key function of government — monitoring of noise abatement policies, when left to the initiative of provincial or municipal authorities, remains limited, and it is thus difficult to make a rigorous assessment of local policy implementation.

3. IMPLEMENTATION OF NATIONAL POLICIES
BY LOCAL AUTHORITIES VARIES CONSIDERABLY

The effort made to implement noise abatement policies, particularly those relating to local noise, varies considerably. This is true not only of the federal countries, where policy definition and implementation vary from state to state or region to region (e.g. Australia and Germany), but also in centralised countries, where local authorities give effect to policies of extremely varied scope depending on their particular sensitivity to noise problems and their priorities in the environmental field. Such diversity can result from several factors:

— The enormous range of noise problems which local authorities have to tackle (scale of transport infrastructures, population density, etc.);
— The awareness and determination of local decision–makers and pressure from the public;
— The training of municipal technical staff responsible for dealing with such issues.

4. HETEROGENEOUS COMPLIANCE WITH REGULATIONS

Much noise abatement policy involves standards and regulations: noise emission limits, soundproofing standards for housing, authorisation procedures for the use of industrial or leisure facilities. Only strict enforcement of such standards and the imposition of penalties when they are not complied with can make regulatory policies effective. But it is clear that enforcement is not always adequate in all countries or for all noise problems. Three examples will illustrate successes and failures in this area.

Industrial plants

In most countries, enforcement of noise regulations for industrial plant is the general rule and is usually effective. This is linked both to the ease with which noise sources can be identified and to prior authorisation procedures, often included in building permits or checks on the environmental impact of industrial plant via inspections. It also seems linked to the industry's investment capability and to its possibilities of taking preventive action, for example when new technologies are introduced (see Part II).

In some countries, such as Japan, catching–up programmes make it possible in time to improve the quality of the noise environment of neighbouring districts. Such programmes may include State assistance with compliance expenditure by industry, such as that involved in the relocation of certain activities where on–site measures prove ineffective or too expensive.

Soundproofing of new buildings

Technical surveillance is also necessary for new buildings along noisy roads. In this case, soundproofing regulations are usually satisfactory from the technical standpoint. However, the training and awareness of those concerned (elected representatives, technical staff, architects and property developers) are often inadequate, at best. Even in a country like the Netherlands, which pursues a very ambitious noise abatement policy, a survey undertaken in 1987 showed that less than 70 per cent of new buildings required by regulations to incorporate top–quality soundproofing complied with the regulations, and only 50 per cent where average soundproofing was necessary.

Urban development near airports

Enforcement of urban development restrictions near airports, designed to limit the number of dwellings or public facilities such as schools or social centres exposed to high noise levels, has proved to be very difficult in most countries.

Clearly, there is a conflict between the wishes of nearby local authorities, who want to maintain urban and economic development in connection with the airport, and the aims of national government, which seeks to apply effective noise abatement policy. The attitudes of the populations concerned are also sometimes contradictory, since, on the one hand, they benefit from the airport facilities and the resulting economic activity while, on the other hand, suffering from the loss of enviromental quality. The likelihood of increasing air traffic in the future and the pressure of urban development offer little hope of any significant and speedy improvement in this area.

5. THE SLOWNESS OF "CATCHING–UP" POLICIES

Although "catching–up" policies (noise screens, better soundproofing) have been implemented in nearly all countries to deal with acute noise problems along main transport

Table 2. **Annual noise abatement expenditure in France**

	1987, million francs
Total public administration	518
of which:	
– noise screens and soundproofing along roads	
• catching-up "black spots"	120
• boulevard périphérique (ring-road, Paris)	60
• new roads	90
– anti-noise brigades	30
Private individuals: soundproofing[a]	1 050
Industry	700
Total	2 268

a) Includes expenditure for thermal insulation.
Source: OECD.

infrastructures (motorways and other roads carrying heavy traffic, railways and airports), in some of them, such programmes are not able to cope with the problems that need to be tackled.

The time horizons envisaged by these programmes for dealing with "black spots" vary greatly. The goal has been set at 15 years in Switzerland; in France, however, the catching–up programme will be spread over several decades, given present budget allocations. In some countries, such programmes account for a considerable share, or even the major portion, of the funds allocated to noise abatement by the authorities. In France, they account for 35 per cent of expenditure by government departments on noise abatement (FF 180 million out of a total of FF 518 million in 1987) (Table 2). In the Netherlands, they represent nearly 60 per cent of expenditure by the Environment Ministry (Gld 69.5 million out of Gld 117.8 million in 1988) (Table 3).

Table 3. **Annual expenditure on noise abatement by ministries[a], Netherlands**

						Expenditures in 10^6 Gld	
	1986	1987	1988	1989	1990	1991	1992
Ministry of the Environment							
1. Research	–	2.0	2.2	2.0	2.1	2.1	2.1
2. Clean technology	5.9	3.8	2.6	2.4	2.4	2.4	2.4
3. Contribution to municipalities	18.3	17.6	17.1	17.4	17.4	17.4	17.4
4. Quiet zones	0.1	0.3	0.1	0.8	0.8	0.8	0.8
5. Road traffic noise	80.7	52.9	69.3	45.8	49.1	49.1	59.3
6. Industrial noise	10.7	20.4	9.0	10.9	11.4	12.4	9.0
7. Railroad noise	1.0	9.9	1.9	3.0	2.8	3.0	3.9
8. Aircraft noise (zoning ac. border)	7.0	7.6	8.7	6.4	6.4	6.4	6.4
9. Other	1.2	1.2	0.8	0.5	0.5	0.7	0.7
10. Non-profit	0.5	1.0	0.6	–	–	–	–
11. Contribution to provinces	10.5	10.4	10.4	10.4	10.4	10.4	10.4
Total	135.9	127.1	122.7	99.6	103.3	104.7	112.4
Ministry of Transport							
1. Railroad noise	4.0	4.0	4.0	4.0	4.0	4.0	4.0
2. Aircraft noise (zoning civil airports)	15.5	15.5	15.5	15.5	15.5	15.5	15.5
Ministry of Defense							
1. Aircraft noise (zoning military airports)	22.0	22.0	22.0	22.0	22.0	22.0	22.0

a) Excludes expenditures by local authorities, industry and households.
Source: Netherlands Ministry of Housing, Planning and Environment.

The key factors determining the success of these catching–up plans seem linked to a large extent to whether funds are allocated for the purpose of increasing the awareness of the authorities and training technical staff responsible for designing and giving effect to the plans. However, even in a country such as Switzerland where the programme is ambitious, time for compliance is relatively short (15 years) and funds are made available by the federal authorities, doubts persist as to whether the additional finance will be available in the long term for the local authorities concerned (cantons and communes).

6. MONITORING IN–SERVICE VEHICLES

Even where they comply with noise emission limits on leaving the factory, motor vehicles can transgress such limits sooner ot later either owing to lack of servicing or because they have been deliberately tampered with (e.g. exhaust pipes). Effective inspection of in–service vehicles is absolutely crucial, but is rarely satisfactory, for lack of resources or lack of political will. Likewise, acoustically certificated aircraft can cause unacceptable disturbance by failing to meet operating rules. However, some countries have been able to establish effective and inexpensive inspection procedures.

Successful experiments with inspection procedures

At Zurich Airport, in Switzerland, checks on take–off paths and noise measurements have been made for many years. Radar follow–up of every take–off and the measurement of noise levels on the ground make it possible to publish monthly lists of airlines whose aircraft violate take–off procedures and paths. Such individual checks are so effective that breaches of take–off procedures have been reduced to less than 0.4 per cent. This has significantly reduced the impact of take–offs on nearby residents. Checks of this kind could probably be applied at all main airports without serious difficulty.

Checks on noise emissions by in–service motor vehicles is another important aspect of enforcement of regulations. Anti–noise brigades are found in several countries, e.g. France and Switzerland, but owing to lack of personnel, are not always highly operational.

The most successful programmes seem to be those being developed in some Australian states, where all vehicles on the road must comply with exhaust noise limits using a "close proximity" test procedure (see Part II, Inset 2). Noisy vehicles may be stopped and tested at the roadside, or may be called in, after repairs, to an agency or privately operated centre for checking. Non–complying vehicles may be subject to further legal actions. These Australian programmes, which are developing slightly differently in each state, use only limited resources but are nevertheless effective. Test results indicate that exhaust noise levels of subject vehicles are reduced on average by 9 dB(A).

Generalising "on–the–spot" checks

Why are on–the–spot checks not generally introduced within the countries concerned and extended to other airports and other towns and regions? To what extent can such experiments be applied to other countries? For example, steps taken at Zurich could presumably also be applied at other airports in other OECD countries. Similarly, on–the–spot checks on motor vehicle noise, as introduced in Australia, are straightforward, effective and inexpensive. The anti–noise brigade operating 24 hours a day in Lausanne (Switzerland) is also simple and efficient. However, it remains to be seen whether co–operation between the police and environmental authorities would be as close in other countries.

In the future, pending what is still the very slow strengthening of standards, policies to control the noise of in–service motor vehicles will be a crucial factor for the successful implementation of policies already adopted and a way of ensuring that the expected benefits of previous tightening of standards will really be obtained.

7. BUDGETARY CHOICES

Budget problems are linked to the definition and implementation of noise abatement policies:

— Policy choices (regulations, incentives, etc.) are rarely backed up by adequate budgetary resources to ensure speedy and widespread application;
— Extra–budgetary funds, such as duties and charges, are still rarely used to finance noise abatement policies (see Chapter 4);
— In several countries, there are gaps in available economic data on noise abatement.

Choices also have to be made in allocating funds as between catching–up policies (abatement) and prevention. In some countries the priority currently being given to catching–up measures and the inadequate political interest in prevention are likely to mean that funds which can be used on abatement become insufficient.

Moreover, there must be systematic efforts to attain some minimum coherence between funds allocated by central or federal government and funds to be provided by regional or local authorities for the effective enforcement of noise abatement measures taken at national level. Most countries today are having some difficulty in reconciling national finances (based on national noise abatement strategy, as in the Netherlands, or through multi–annual plans, as in Switzerland) with the finances of territorial authorities over which central government has far less control — or none at all — as regards volume, regularity and consistency over time. In some countries, therefore, concern is felt: will it continue to be possible to find the funds necessary to pursue ambitious noise abatement policies adopted and partly financed by central government?

Lastly, funds allocated to noise abatement come from different origins: the general State budget, noise charges and duties. Funds which are "specifically allocated" (i.e. related in one way or another to noise sources, their use or their harmful effects) and which do not have to be renegotiated each year when budgets are prepared, have proved their effectiveness. This is the case with the petrol tax in the Netherlands and Switzerland (see Part II). It is also true of take–off charges for aircraft which go to pay for soundproofing and other works near some airports, e.g. in France. But in most cases noise abatement policies still depend almost entirely on government budgets, particularly since such taxes have recently been challenged in some countries.

8. TRAFFIC MANAGEMENT AND NOISE REDUCTION: UNEVEN RESULTS

Management of road traffic and of urban transport in general is a key instrument in reducing disamenity caused by motor vehicles. But the success achieved depends on the approach adopted.

Road traffic control and management policies, which rely solely on measures affecting vehicle speeds and traffic fluidity to reduce noise levels, do not seem capable of attaining the sought–after objectives, except on limited stretches of roads or in certain districts: considerable resources are committed, implemented and monitored but to little effect. On the other hand, traffic plans designed to distribute traffic throughout the existing or newly created road network, in such a way as to protect quiet districts while concentrating nuisance on a few main routes, are more effective.

Environment Ministries in Switzerland and the Netherlands use computers to devise traffic models and determine resulting noise levels along any road together with levels of air pollution. These models make it possible to test various traffic distribution strategies and allow for noise as a criterion of decision–making along with other environmental factors.

However, the most promising solutions are traffic restrictions affecting noisy vehicles, principally lorries: the latter cannot be used at certain times (e.g. at night) or in certain areas (e.g. town centres or residential districts) (see Chapter 5).

Some countries, such as the Netherlands, also plan to adopt much stricter policies intended to reduce traffic volume in towns; these policies will be based on a global approach to urban and regional transport management and will integrate management of all transport modes, including public transport, and introduce road pricing for private individuals. This approach stems from the realisation that the numbers of private cars and lorries are likely to grow and that any policy to combat transport noise has to be closely co–ordinated (or "integrated") with overall transport policy, making proper allowance for all environmental factors.

Chapter 4

ECONOMIC INCENTIVES

1. DEFINITION AND OBJECTIVES

Economic instruments back up the range of tools (standards and regulations in particular) available to policy–makers. They consist essentially of various taxes and charges on products or sources of pollution.

Economic instruments rarely replace direct regulation; more often the choice is between various combinations of the two. In practice an empirical approach seems to predominate: economic instruments thus back up direct regulations as part of mixed systems. In such combinations economic instruments are intended to provide the funds needed to finance environmental protection measures, improve the application of direct regulations to which they are linked, and stimulate technical innovation. Direct regulation is retained since it makes it possible to influence the behaviour of actors, provided it is effectively enforced[8].

2. INSTRUMENTS USED IN CONNECTION WITH NOISE ABATEMENT

Several types of incentives and economic instruments are used in OECD countries in connection with noise abatement (see Part II). The six countries covered by the case studies currently make use of three types of economic instrument (Table 4):

— Charges on noise sources;
— Financial aids;
— Special taxes on products.

Compared to the situation analysed a few years ago[9] and in spite of the OECD Recommendation of 1985, the use of economic instruments for purposes of noise abatement has not significantly increased in recent years. It has even declined in some countries. Examples are the charge on aircraft noise in France which was abolished in 1987 on purely legal grounds, and the financial aids previously paid to manufacturers of road transport goods vehicles, in France and Japan, in the form of grants or loans for research and development. In the Netherlands, several charges for various types of pollution and nuisance (including noise) were found to be effective but too complicated to administer. In 1988 a new general tax on fuels replaced the noise charge payable by industrial establishments (introduced in 1981) and the special tax on motor vehicle fuel.

Table 4.

Table 4. **Economic instruments in noise abatement**

Six countries studied

Type of incentive	Noise source	Objective[a]	Countries and when implemented	Target group or area of application
Charges	Aircraft	F	Japan (1975)[e]	Airlines
		F	France (1973 to 1984)[f]	Paris Airports
		F, I	France (1984 to 1987)	Paris Airports
		F	Netherlands (1983)	Airlines
		F, I	Switzerland (1980)	Airlines (30 European airports only)
	Industrial establishment	F	Netherlands (1983 to 1988)	Leading industrial companies
Financial aids	Road vehicles	R&D finance	France (1971 to 1988) Japan (1974 to 1978) Australia[d] Germany	Renault V.I. (subsidies) 4 manufacturers (loans) Tax reduction for R&D
		Help with purchase of low-noise vehicle	Germany (1981) (1988)[b] Netherlands (1981) (1988)[b]	Goods transport by road[c] Goods transport by road
Reduction on landing tax	Aircraft	I	Germany (1980)	Airlines
Special taxes			Netherlands (never applied)	Noisy vehicles
Special fuel tax			Netherlands (1982 to 1988)	All users
General fuel tax			Netherlands (1988) and Switzerland (1985)	All users, also used for other environmental problems

a) F = Finance; I = Incentive.
b) First implemented in 1981 and substantially amended in 1988.
c) Two towns only: Berlin and Bad Reichenhall (25 vehicles in the latter).
d) Not at present used for noise.
e) Programme or action started in 1975 and still continuing.
f) Programme or action started in 1973 and stopped in 1984.
Source: OECD.

This trend is surprising since, in other areas of environmental protection (air, water, waste, etc.), use made of economic instruments has increased considerably over the past ten years. Charges paid in respect of noise, for example, amount to ECU 6 million in France, while charges for water are ECU 240 million, i.e. 40 times as much. The same figures for the Netherlands are ECU 14 million and ECU 473 million respectively.

Except for the Netherlands, where the fuel tax affects all land transport vehicles, economic instruments increasingly affect only a small proportion of noise sources, primarily aircraft. What is more, these instruments usually have no incentive character and are therefore today mainly ways of obtaining additional funds to support noise abatement policies.

Charges on aircraft noise

This non–existent or very small incentive element is particularly noticeable in connection with charges concerning aircraft: the sums at stake and the abatements or reductions of landing charges in respect of noise are out of proportion to the costs of using the aircraft and thus give airlines very little incentive to change. On the other hand, charges do make it possible in most of the countries where they are used to fund soundproofing (of housing, schools, social facilities, etc.) needed in the most exposed areas around airports. However, they affect only 30 airports in Europe, all of them civil airports, while they are adopted at most of the civil airports in Japan (see Part II).

Economic instruments and "low–noise" vehicles

Financial aids in the form of grants or individual loans to help R&D on low–noise vehicles by private manufacturers, were quite widespread in in Japan in the 1970s and in France and Germany in the 1980s. They are still available today in the latter country (see Part II). They made a considerable contribution to the development by several manufacturers of goods vehicles or private cars with noise levels significantly below current standards.

Today, discussion in Europe is focusing on air pollution. As a result, the R&D effort necessary to devise quieter vehicles meeting the OECD recommendations of 1980[10] (below 75 dB(A) for private cars and below 80 dB(A) for lorries) is to be overlooked, precisely at a time when these recommendations need to be tightened up if the acoustic environment is to be improved. Therefore, renewed incentives to research into the design and marketing of quieter vehicles are badly needed. The long–term objective — to be achieved by 2005-2010 — should be 70 dB(A) for cars and 75 dB(A) for lorries, i.e. 5 dB(A) below the 1980 recommendations. Such a target seems technically feasible if the preparatory work done and proposals put forward by the Netherlands are accepted[11]. With such target levels, tyre/road noise will be an increasing problem and therefore it will be necessary to develop emission limits related to tyre noise at the same time.

A market for low–noise vehicles also has to be created. This can be done by strengthening standards and by incentives for the use of vehicles which are quieter than required by current standards. The economic interests involved and competition in the field of transport are such that, in the absence of economic incentives for the purchase of low–noise vehicles, there is no demand for them since they (lorries in particular) are more costly both to purchase and to operate. On the other hand, there is a market for quieter buses, either because local authorities include them as one of the objectives of their policy for the quality of the urban environment, or because governments encourage the purchase of such vehicles.

Assistance with the purchase of low–noise vehicles for goods transport is at present found in only two countries, Germany and the Netherlands. The system of incentives used in the Netherlands since 1981, involving grants for the purchase of vehicles quieter than current standards, is considered extremely efficient. At the same time, it is contrary to the Polluter–Pays–Principle. More than 60 per cent of lorries in use in the Netherlands thus have noise levels 5 dB(A) below current standards. This scheme was part of a larger general investment subsidy programme which was later abolished for general budgetary reasons. A special investment subsidy programme remained: Gld 6.75 million was available for low–noise lorries (see Part II, Inset 3).

The system in Germany is applied solely at local level in two towns, Berlin and Bad Reichenhall (see Part II, Inset 4). In the last town it affects only 25 vehicles, but is co–ordinated with policies of restricting traffic at certain times (night–time) and in certain areas (town centre and residential districts for noisy lorries), thus ensuring consistency and effectiveness at local level. This is however far short of any general application to the 1.3 million goods vehicles on the roads throughout the country.

In the absence of more coherent and determined government policies, it is to be feared that vehicle manufacturers will not undertake sufficient R&D to design and market low–noise vehicles, even if they are given assistance in doing so. Private carriers, if not encouraged to buy quieter vehicles, will in all probability continue to purchase vehicles which simply comply with existing standards.

Political determination and the coherence of action taken — including the definite likelihood of stricter standards, local policies restricting or filtering traffic, and incentives of various kinds to discourage noisy vehicles and encourage low–noise ones — are therefore the key factors determining the real long–term effectiveness of economic incentives to the use of quieter vehicles (see also Chapter 5 below for non–economic incentives).

3. LITTLE USED BUT PROMISING POTENTIAL

Although economic instruments are not used extensively in several countries and are even, in some cases, now being abandoned, they do have considerable potential for effective noise abatement policies. In the first place, these instruments are effective ways of providing finance and comply with the Polluter–Pays–Principle (except for subsidies not covered by the relevant charges)[12]. They can also act as effective incentives to the use or production of quieter vehicles, provided they are co–ordinated and consistent with other tools at the disposal of government and form part of ambitious long–term policies (stricter standards, selective restrictions on the use of vehicles, taxes on noisy vehicles).

It is therefore necessary to take several steps:

— Extend the use of economic instruments for purposes of noise abatement in countries which have little or no recourse to them;
— Relate them where possible to the use of noisy products rather than to the purchase of such products;
— Graduate incentives in proportion to actual nuisance levels;
— In particular, extend their application to the largest possible number of noise sources, including private cars and two–wheeled vehicles.

Chapter 5

NON–ECONOMIC INCENTIVES

1. DEFINITION AND OBJECTIVES

Admittedly noise abatement depends primarily on regulations. But regulations are generally inadequate for several reasons:

— Regulations do not resolve all problems, particularly where behaviour is the primary factor underlying noise problems;
— The provisions of laws and regulations are not always strict enough and enforcement in particular is inadequate; enforcement is rarely uniform throughout the national territory;
— Regulations, which are by their very nature inflexible, change slowly and often come to be ill–adapted or inadequate to cope with changing noise problems.

Most noise abatement policies now being applied therefore include incentives in order to back up regulations or to replace them when necessary.

Alongside economic instruments — taxes, charges — which play or could play an important persuasive and financing role, countries also use non–economic incentives. Unlike regulations, these do not impose obligations; and unlike economic instruments, they do not offer or remove any monetary benefits.

These non–economic incentives try to encourage low–noise behaviour, stimulate the production, purchase and use of quiet products and vehicles and promote allowance for noise in action taken and future planning. The targets of non–economic incentives are the general public or specific groups (elected representatives, technical staff, etc.), products, and present or future in decision–making.

2. USE OF NON–ECONOMIC INCENTIVES: STILL LIMITED

In general, in the countries studied, non–economic incentives still occupy a limited place in noise abatement policies. Indeed, most countries base their efforts primarily on noise abatement at source by means of regulations and investment programmes, particularly as regards catching–up policies (infrastructure, noise screens, soundproofing).

All of the countries studied use non–economic incentives but on differing scales (Table 5). No country appears to use all those that are available, although the Netherlands

Table 5. **Noise abatement incentives**

Six countries studied

Target	TYPE OF INCENTIVE		Countries concerned
	Scope	Type of project	
Individuals	General	– Noise abatement campaign	Netherlands, Japan, Switzerland, Australia, France, Germany
		– Creation of public information services (documentation, legal assistance, exhibitions, films, etc.)	France, Netherlands, Switzerland, Germany
	Targeted at specific population groups	– Promoting understanding and awareness by children and teenagers	France, Netherlands
		– Decision-makers:	
		• training of representatives and officials	France, Netherlands, Switzerland
		• training and informing staff	France, Netherlands, Switzerland
		• "pilot town" projects	France, Japan
Products	Product information	– Labelling	Germany, Australia, Netherlands
		– Acoustic quality certificate	Germany, France, Switzerland
	Products use	– Advertising of low-noise products	Switzerland, Netherlands
		– Local and national government procurement policy	Germany, France, Netherlands
		– Restriction of use of noisy products	Germany
Projects	Planning	– Impact study: diagnosis of noise situation	France, Netherlands, Switzerland, Germany, Japan, Australia
		– Traffic plan	France, Netherlands, Switzerland, Germany, Japan, Australia
	General	– Anti-noise brigades	Switzerland, France, Australia
		– Creation of consultation bodies	France, Netherlands, Australia

Source: "Fighting Noise", OECD, Paris, 1986, updated by reference to the six case studies.

and, to a lesserextent, France, Germany and Switzerland do use a number of them. Lastly, since some of these incentives are applied on the initiative of local authorities, rather than by central government alone, the use made of them can vary considerably within a given country.

3. AN ESSENTIAL ROLE

Non–economic incentives are used primarily in connection with promoting awareness of the problem and providing information and training. They fulfil an essential function in this area and help to make regulations acceptable and comprehensible to the population groups concerned.

People who are conscious of the problem are more prepared to accept regulations which might otherwise seem superfluous or unpalatable. When information is provided, the possible disadvantages of comprehensive noise abatement policy, which inevitably entails constraints, prohibitions and restrictions, are better understood and less likely to encounter opposition. The public and decision–makers are made aware of the cost of damage caused by noise, and thus of the possible benefits of noise abatement.

Non–economic incentives are also an essential adjunct to policy implementation and enforcement of regulations.

The experience of Switzerland, with its system of local democracy, public participation in the definition of policy objectives and provision of the funds necessary, is a good illustration of the fundamental role of public information and awareness in setting up an ambitious noise abatement policy. Conversely, in some other countries, the rather limited motivation of elected representatives and local technical staff leads to widely varying and generally very limited use of regulatory instruments provided by central government and available in principle for noise abatement.

4. TRAINING OF TECHNICAL STAFF AND ELECTED REPRESENTATIVES

Many aspects of noise abatement policies depend on action at local or regional level. However, detailed and precise they may be, regulations adopted at national level will remain a dead letter unless applied by hundreds or thousands of local personnel who on a day–to–day basis prepare technical documentation, initiate works, plan local development, supervise private projects (e.g. building permits for housing or industrial plant) and enforce noise regulations (policing of drivers and residents).

Awareness of noise problems on the part of technical staff and elected representatives is essential to the success of abatement policies. Few countries, however, have really committed themselves to programmes to train and increase the awareness of these essential groups.

It is not easy to define precise objectives for the training of decision–makers, nor in particular to define and apply means of measuring performance following such training; but it would seem that, in most countries, only a small proportion of such needs are met. Yet — to transpose the situation — would an industrialist who planned to change the production processes in his factories or adopt a new marketing strategy hesitate to put the necessary funds into retraining his workers and technical and sales staff?

But the fact is that few of those locally responsible for town–planning policies have any real training or awareness in respect of noise problems and few officials have the technical knowledge needed to give effect to noise abatement policies with competence and efficiency. Furthermore, technicians or officials involved in noise abatement policies often have other responsibilities. In many cases, it is far more efficient to create a specialised workforce for noise abatement; otherwise, noise is often treated as secondary to other local government objectives, or is simply overlooked. Too few towns can claim to have made proper allowance for noise in preparing traffic plans alongside other assessment and decision–making criteria (urban planning and development, traffic management, choice of mode, form of operation, accessibility, air pollution).

Experience also shows that noise is very inadequately taken into account in land–use policies. Analysis of urban planning policies, for example near airports or along the noisiest roads in France or Japan, reveals very real shortcomings in this area, whereas in the same countries, noise is now given more attention in studies for major new transport links (motorways, urban freeways, high–speed rail links).

To remedy this failing some countries (e.g. Australia, Germany, the Netherlands and Switzerland) are now taking more deliberate steps to combat noise in urban planning and in the control of urban development; these are based primarily on special noise zoning and quality objectives for the acoustic environment depending on types of district. It remains to be seen whether such measures, which are very sophisticated in procedural terms and require great political determination on the part of local authorities, will be satisfactorily implemented in all towns.

5. EDUCATING THE PUBLIC

In all countries campaigns to educate the public are seen as an essential policy instrument and a vital part of policy implementation and effectiveness (see Part II). However, the experience of several countries (Australia, Japan, the Netherlands and Switzerland) suggests that it is better to organise ongoing campaigns of limited scope, giving regular backing to advances in noise abatement (e.g. the introduction of new regulations or a new policy), rather than major but occasional and short–lived national campaigns, unrelated to progress achieved and with no lasting effect.

Moreover, experience in countries, such as Japan and Switzerland, has shown that campaigns undertaken locally to inform the public and increase awareness are more effective than national campaigns. The way they are undertaken is also important. In several countries (e.g. France and the Netherlands), national information and promotion campaigns are organised by private bodies. The role that such private or non–profit associations can thus play, both nationally and locally, makes it possible to avoid having the public view such campaigns as a kind of regimentation. What is more, since such bodies are relatively close to the public, they have a good understanding of the target groups and can tailor their information policies accordingly.

6. LOCAL "PILOT" PROJECTS

Experiments with local authorities in mind have proved effective in some countries. In France, "pilot projects for quiet towns" have led 25 towns to sign contracts with the State whereby they agree to give effect to a specific programme of practical noise abatement, with the State bearing half the cost (see Part II, Inset 6).

In the Netherlands, the Environment Ministry provides those towns which so wish with both computer facilities and the necessary funds to allow for noise in urban road traffic management. Similar models are also to be found in Switzerland.

Incentive programmes of this kind, which aim to mobilise and motivate local authorities and local councillors and provide them with technical assistance, are a good way of testing their ability to give effect to noise abatement policy at local level. An initial evaluation of such efforts in specifically chosen towns will then enable central government to adopt more appropriate and more coherent policies at national level. The programmes also have the advantage of setting an example for other local authorities.

7. PROMOTION OF LOW–NOISE PRODUCTS

Non–economic incentives for the use of "low–noise" products, in particular products which are quieter than required by current norms, comprise various elements such as information, labelling and promotion or, conversely, restrictions on the use of noisy products or devices. They back up economic incentives and regulations.

The labelling of low–noise products is a comparatively inexpensive way of better informing consumers and users, and may persuade them to change their purchasing behaviour. At the same time, it helps encourage firms to market products in line with consumer demand. The labelling of low–noise products is very little used at present, except in Germany for goods vehicles and products bearing the "environment–friendly" label. The label has been introduced for products which respect the environment, in the light of various criteria such as pollutant emission, waste generation, energy consumption and noise level. Noise labelling has also been introduced over the last several years in some Australian states, for products such as domestic air conditioners, motorised lawn–mowers and pavement breakers/air compressors (see Part II).

Other incentives resemble regulations insofar as it is usually by means of regulations that towns restrict the local use of noisy products or vehicles at certain times and in certain areas while exempting low–noise products and vehicles. In Germany, for example, low–noise lorries are authorised to cross town centres or travel at night, while lorries without the "low–noise" label are prohibited (see Part II).

Purely national or local policies to promote low–noise products may act as obstacles to trade and influence markets. For this reason co–ordination is desirable at international level in relation to:

— Standardization of methods of acoustic measurement;
— Easy recognition of marks or labels;

— Identical quality levels in different countries; and, in particular,

— Close co–ordination with other types of low–noise incentives (purchasing price subsidies, taxes on noisy products, restrictions on use of noisy products and exemption from restrictions for low–noise products).

Various measures would make it possible to introduce in a coherent way a real policy to promote low–noise vehicles or goods in the OECD countries, or in a smaller group of countries such as the European Community (Table 6).

Table 6 . **Measures to encourage low-noise commercial vehicles towards the year 2000**

Short-term targets	Medium and long-term targets
* **Define "low-noise"** • new vehicles • in-service vehicles (Scope: whole OECD)	* **Labelling for low-noise products** • based on definitions (Scope: whole OECD or EC schemes)
* **Educate the public** • decibel scale • what can be achieved (Scope: whole OECD)	* **Establish European framework for environmental traffic management fully compatible with EC/ECE type approvals system** • based on definitions • clear legal basis (Scope: particularly EC)
* **Extend environmental traffic management schemes** • "low-noise" new vehicle exemptions • "low-noise" vehicle exemptions for in-service vehicles. (Scope: whole OECD)	* **Vehicle tax rates to include noise charge** • through EC single market provisions (Scope: particularly EC)
	* **Emission limits** • work towards lower limits based on 'low-noise" definitions (Scope: whole OECD)
	* **Research and development support** • develop programme for support of future "low-noise" vehicle targets • include linkage with tyre-road noise to maximise impacts of vehicle improvements. (Scope: whole OECD)

8. CONTROLLING AND GENERALISING USE OF INSTRUMENTS

Non–economic incentives are today accepted as being not only useful but often essential if noise abatement is to be successful.

When used to back up an ambitious noise abatement policy, they help, by informing the public and increasing awareness, to make the need for such a policy better understood and reduce the risk of its being rejected. By means of programmes to train technical staff and decision–makers and increase their awareness of the problem, they help improve the implementation of noise abatement policies and their enforcement at local level.

Much remains to be done: as regards products, in various countries, special efforts should be made to analyse in depth the coherence of non–economic incentives (labelling, certification, publicity, restrictions on use) with economic incentives, on the one hand, and regulations, on the other. This study and analysis clearly has to be undertaken at international level if it is to have any chance of leading to some practical action.

Two essential problems are:

— How to ensure that these incentives are applied generally? This probably depends on making the right resources available (budgetary, technical and trained staff); and
— How to measure the performance and effectiveness of these incentives in promoting training and increasing public awareness?

Although the behaviour of technical staff can be changed fairly easily through technical and methodological training, altering the attitudes and behaviour of the public and decision–makers, especially of elected representatives, is much more difficult, and the situation has still not been properly analysed.

The discrepancy observed in most countries between the importance attached to noise by the public and the low priority given to noise abatement by those who decide policy is a good example of this difficulty. One promising analytical approach might be to link noise abatement more closely to three topics which receive more widespread attention, i.e. improved safety, energy saving and air pollution control.

Chapter 6

CONCLUSIONS

In the light of the above analysis, it is possible to draw a number of conclusions regarding future trends and noise abatement policies, and to propose possible directions for action to strengthen such policies and more particularly improve their implementaton.

1. NOISE PROBLEMS IN THE YEARS AHEAD

The increase in numbers of noise sources in the years ahead and the growing expectations of the public are likely, in most OECD countries, to make noise problems more acute in the longer term. Sources of noise (road traffic, air traffic, domestic appliances, hi–fi equipment, etc.) will also, in many cases, become increasingly powerful. Potential noise generated will thus be all the greater, failing appropriate technological solutions or stricter regulations. In addition, sources will probably be dispersed over ever–larger areas, in the countryside, nature and leisure areas, and will also increasingly spread over time, throughout the day, evenings, nights and weekends. The most important cause of change, however, seems to be the increase in mobility and the growing number of vehicles and other devices, primarily on the roads and in the air, but also where rail is concerned in some countries.

Everything, therefore, seems to bear out the pessimistic forecasts based on scenarios and models developed in some countries in the early 1980s which indicated that, in the absence of ambitious policies, the acoustic environment was likely to remain unsatisfactory or even deteriorate still further[13]. New scenarios, forecasts and outlooks are necessary for the beginning of the 1990s so as to provide policy guidance. Statistics on the current state of the acoustic environment have certain shortcomings; a similar situation is also emerging in relation to forecasts.

Lastly, it is to be expected that public demands for a better quality environment and a quieter environment will increase, in line with the general trend in public expectations concerning the environment and the quality of life; this is a consequence of the probable rise in standards of education and the probable trend towards more stressful lifestyles (more urban development, denser traffic, etc.).

2. ASSESSMENT OF POLICIES IN THE LIGHT
OF THE OECD'S WORK AND RECOMMENDATION

The conclusions of the OECD's work undertaken as of 1985–86 provide a reference by which to assess the strengthening of noise abatement policies and the improvement of their implementation:

"Clear and precise objectives, a flexible but real inflection of behaviour, encouragement for local action together with national and international surveillance, and sustained self–financing mechanisms through economic instruments seem to be the means for obtaining a satisfactory noise environment. Such an environment is an essential factor in the quality of life."[14]

In the light of these conclusions, supported by the Recommendation adopted by the Council of the OECD in 1985, little real progress seems to have been made in recent years. Genuine national strategies to fight noise have been established only in the Netherlands and Switzerland. In most other countries, the advances that have been made are mostly confined to specific cases or limited to specific sources (e.g. allowance for noise in new transport infrastructures, checks on noise in fixed plant, surveillance of aircraft noise at some airports, and anti–noise brigades). Admittedly, catching–up programmes (soundproofing, noise screens, etc.) have been implemented but are far from having dealt with all the "black spots". Where economic instruments are concerned, the Netherlands and Switzerland have introduced incentives to purchase low–noise vehicles and taxes to finance noise abatement policies.

But shortcomings and failures remain widespread with regard to the control of neighbourhood noise and of in–service vehicles; allowance for noise problems in urban planning; motivating and training those involved at local level and supervising them; and the limited or even declining use made of economic incentives and the inadequate use of non–economic incentives.

3.   THE NEED FOR STRENGTHENED AND CO–ORDINATED POLICIES

The OECD countries must resolutely commit themselves to strengthening their noise abatement policies on the basis of the following six points:

i.   Develop a real national strategy co–ordinated with local and regional levels

This implies:
— A clear definition of objectives, quantified wherever possible;
— The explicit distribution of responsibilities among the various public actors;
— Linking the objectives to be attained and the resources needed to guarantee complete and gradual implementation. In particular, this means greater supervision, finance and incentives of all kinds;
— Acknowledging the need for a coherent and co–ordinated approach to noise policy by public authorities at all levels.

A national strategy will often be implemented locally by the national, State or local public administration. Since many aspects of noise abatement policies depend on the local situation, components of noise policies often have to be defined locally.

There is a need for improved knowledge and assessment of the development, implementation, performance, and current shortcomings of local noise policies developed by local authorities throughout OECD countries.

ii. Provide the resources needed for effective implementation of policies and regulations

Policies and regulations will remain a dead letter unless appropriate resources are provided. In the absence of proper enforcement and penalties, many standards (e.g. soundproofing of buildings) are ignored. Not only must the often meagre resources allocated to policy implementation be increased, but steps must also be taken to increase their efficiency, for instance through simplified procedures for measuring noise "on the spot", participation by the private sector (e.g. fitters of exhaust pipes) and by the public, incentives (see below), etc.

iii. Provide the resources and tools to assess policy implementation

In some countries analysis of noise abatement has brought out the widespread absence of any policy assessment, particularly where policies are defined and applied locally. Only when express provision is made for such assessment at the time policies are drawn up and when the necessary resources are specifically identified and allocated for this purpose can assessment of the effectiveness of noise abatement policies become a reality and appropriate changes be made to the policies in the future.

iv. Generalise the use of incentive policies

Economic incentives for noise reduction are still used less than incentives in other environmental areas. They have nevertheless shown their effectiveness in cases where they have been used. Much more general use should therefore be made of such incentives: charges and taxes, financial aids, special purpose taxes, etc. It would be appropriate to tax the use of products rather than their acquisition and to extend charges to cover the greatest possible number of noise sources.

v. Act vigorously to change the behaviour of the public and of decision–makers

In most cases, public support for noise abatement policies, which depends on the level of awareness of those affected, and application of policies at local level, depending primarily on the motivation of local decision–makers, can be improved only by vigorous efforts to change behaviour.

Non–economic incentives will play a fundamental role in the likely event that some regulations undergo little change.

vi. Strengthen noise emission standards for vehicles

The fact that "low–noise" vehicles are already available shows that the strengthening of emission standards for vehicles is possible. It will be increasingly necessary as numbers of vehicles and mobility increase. In view of the time it takes to investigate, negotiate and introduce new standards, the process of tightening up emission standards needs to be set in motion immediately, particularly for goods vehicles. Long–term targets (by 2005–2010) could be *70 dB(A) for private cars and 75 dB(A) for lorries and buses.*

NOTES AND REFERENCES

1. Other types of noise from fixed sources, such as industrial noise, are not included in the assessment, primarily because few comparable statistics are available for the OECD area and also because such problems are of more limited importance.

2. OECD (1989), "OECD Environmental Data, Compendium 1989", Paris.

3. Decibel (dB): unit of measure of sound pressure level related to a standard reference level of 0.00002 Newtons per square metre. The decibel scale is logarithmic so that a very wide range of audible sound can be described in terms of a manageably small range of numerical expressions. A sound of 0 dB would be just audible to a person with good hearing. A sound of 120 dB would cause pain in the ear. The acoustical pressure of the second is one million times greater than that of the first.

   Decibel (A–weighted)(dB(A)): a measure of sound in which greater emphasis is given to medium and high frequencies to which the human ear is most sensitive. The dB(A) measure, which is the most usual in noise abatement and control activities, gives a good correlation with the subjective impression of loudness (an addition of 10 dB(A) represents approximately a doubling of subjective loudness).

   Equivalent continuous sound level (Leq): a level of constant sound (in dBA) which would have the same sound energy over a given period as the measured fluctuating sound under consideration.

4. The stricter limits which came into force at the end of the 1980s (1988 in the EC countries, for example) produce results only in the long term, as vehicles are replaced, and only provided they are not offset by a sharp upturn in traffic.

5. The Noise Abatement Act adopted by Parliament in 1979 and fully applied as from 1st July 1987.

6. Federal Act for the Protection of the Environment of 1983 in force from 1st January 1985; Ordinance on noise published in 1986 and in force as from April 1987.

7. OECD (1987), "Improving the Enforcement of Environmental Policies", Paris.

8. OECD (1989), "Economic Instruments for Environmental Protection", Paris.

9. OECD (1986), "Fighting Noise", Paris.

10. "Fighting Noise", *op. cit.*

11. "Reorientation of Noise Policy on Appliances", TNO report No. 621.001 of 16th September 1988.

12. "Economic Instruments for Environmental Protection", *op. cit.*

13. "Fighting Noise", *op. cit.*

14. "Fighting Noise", *op. cit.*

Part II

AN EXAMINATION OF NOISE ABATEMENT POLICIES IN SIX COUNTRIES

Chapter 1

OVERALL POLICY FRAMEWORK FOR NOISE ABATEMENT

1. EXPOSURE TO NOISE NUISANCE

Previous OECD work has reported the thresholds for noise nuisance as follows:

— 55–60 dB(A)[1] noise creates annoyance and disturbs sleep;
— At 60–65 dB(A) annoyance increases considerably;
— At above 65 dB(A) constrained behaviour patterns, symptomatic of serious damage caused by noise, arise.

OECD has estimated that, in the early 1980s, more than 130 million people in its Member countries were exposed to noise levels in excess of 65 dB(A), most of which is attributed to road vehicles[2].

However, the major problems of noise are perceived differently from country to country based on several factors including:

— Population density;
— The degree of urbanisation and proximity of noise–generating installations (e.g. roads, airports, railways, factories) to residential areas;
— Car ownership levels and extent of road networks in relation to provision of mass rapid transit.

Thus, a high level of attention has focused on railway noise in Japan, aircraft noise in Switzerland and road traffic noise in Germany and the Netherlands. In France, more complaints arise from identifiable domestic and industrial sources than from road and traffic noise. Broadly speaking, the concerns expressed in the different countries about different sources of noise nuisance dictate policies which have been used to address the problem in those countries.

2. POLICY MEASURES FOR NOISE ABATEMENT

Policies developed at international, national and local levels

— Actions to restrict noise emissions at source and set noise limits tend to be determined at international level, particularly in Europe and particularly for heavily traded products, e.g. vehicles, aircraft;
— Policies which establish ambient noise targets and adopt a comprehensive approach to reducing people's exposure to noise tend, where this approach exists, to be

51

developed by national governments, or state governments in federated countries, e.g. Australia;

— Much of the activity designed to ameliorate the impact of noise in the case study countries is carried out by local authorities. This includes planning measures and barriers to situate noise–generating activities at some distance from residential/leisure areas, as well as education programmes and legal sanctions taking a variety of forms.

The types of action taken by each of these levels of government are reviewed below.

International action

Steps have been taken by international organisations (notably ECE and EC) in the form of agreed emission limits for new products in the following areas:

— Motor vehicles (heavy and light commercial vehicles, buses, cars, motorcycles and mopeds);
— Aircraft;
— Construction equipment and various industrial and domestic movable plant and equipment.

Tests are carried out on prototypes which are designed to meet the noise emissions targets for the product, based on weight and power, by a margin of at least 2 dB(A); this allows for standard deviations in noise levels of vehicles or equipment coming off the production line. Once the prototype has received type approval, there is no necessity for further testing of individual models.

Regulations have been successful in reducing emissions from major sources of noise. For example, international agreements led to reductions of some 3 dB(A) per vehicle in noise emissions from heavy vehicles between 1972 and 1980 and a further reduction of 3 dB(A) with the introduction of the latest EC regulations.

There are, nevertheless, drawbacks in relying on international regulations as the basis of noise abatement policy. Negotiation of international legislation involves long time–lags and even when new limits have been implemented the noise levels of the whole fleet of vehicles will not be affected until low–noise designs replace all existing products. In the case of heavy goods vehicles or aircraft, this can take many years.

For countries which give the greatest priority to noise abatement, international harmonization can be experienced as a barrier to effective policy action. These countries follow comprehensive noise abatement approaches in order to pre–empt delays and ensure that manufacturers and operators have incentives to abate noise at source. Some countries have introduced a range of additional actions which also try to influence the volume of noise sources, in addition to emissions from individual sources. This is probably the area in which differences between countries with the most energetic noise control policies and other countries are most apparent. In the future, policies may vary even more radically as some countries concentrate on trying to limit absolute volumes of private road traffic while other countries encourage the use of low–noise products. These differences are discussed briefly in the following section and in more detail in subsequent chapters.

National noise abatement framework

In several of the case study countries, all sources of noise are considered potentially problematic and comprehensive, and noise abatement legislation provides a full framework for national strategy for acting on all types of noise at source. This is the case in Japan and the Netherlands, where environmental quality standards form the basis of policy. The approach is general, although some sources of noise may be covered by acts aimed at transport rather than by acts aimed at noise as such.

In other countries, noise abatement legislation has grown in a piecemeal fashion. This may mean that additional sectoral actions are developed ad hoc directly on the basis of the type and extent of complaints as they become subjectively important (one example is the current work on railway noise in France), or that legislation is applied mainly at regional or state level while local incentives are gradually co–ordinated and harmonized by national bodies (as has happened in Australia and Germany).

In some countries, noise legislation may be comprehensive at local levels, irrespective of the national context. This is the case in federated countries, such as Australia, where different states have different noise abatement priorities. On the other hand, local implementation and financing of noise abatement means that local politicians will actively pursue abatement policies only where the costs of noise damage in terms of sleep and stress are well recognised. In France, the diversity of organisations involved is so great, with some five hundred urban communes having responsibility for noise policy, that decision–making and implementation are severely hindered. Local responsibility for both implementation and finance may be a strength (as in German spa towns) or a weakness (as in French "quiet towns").

Focus of policies

The in approach used in terms of the responsible authorities, legislative framework and focus of activity, varies considerably among the case study countries (Table 1). Variations in policy orientation may be briefly summarised as follows:

— In Australia, policy tends to be fragmented because action is at the state level. In general, most policy is introduced in reaction to complaints and consequently policies are "scattered", with no specific co–ordination. The more populous states have tended to be the leaders in introducing labelling for products, standards for new motor vehicles, testing in–service vehicles and industry and planning controls and in raising public awareness of the noise issue. These are relatively low–cost options which may be pursued at local or international level;

— In France, the legal framework separates planning powers, which are held at local level, from financial powers for raising charges and subsidies, at a national level. Policy has tended to centre on integrated action at a municipal level, particularly focusing on traffic restraint, land use planning and raising public awareness;

— In Germany, policy at local level concentrates on traffic restraint schemes aimed at simultaneously reducing noise and air immissions. Germany has been the leader in developing products which meet requirements more stringent than the international requirements. Positive action focuses on providing incentives for operators to use low–noise products, and so creating self–sustaining markets;

— Japanese policy is consistent in approach to industrial, air, rail and road traffic noise. It strives to reduce both noise at source through emission standards and receptor noise, and to target Environmental Quality Standards with an emphasis on zoning, noise barriers and insulation. Railway noise is approached in a more comprehensive manner than in other countries;

— The Netherlands has the most integrated policy framework, based on zoning around fixed installations alongside roads and railways and around airports, and a system of charges and subsidies to abate noise at source: e.g. subsidies for low–noise vehicles, charges for noisy installations and a fuel charge for vehicles. The Netherlands has expressed the intention of reducing future traffic growth by 20 per cent (using road pricing, etc.) as the only way of meeting environmental quality objectives and reducing noise emission levels of motor vehicles (cars and motorcycles) to 70 dB(A) and heavy vehicles to 75 dB(A);

— Switzerland has been the leader in limiting traffic noise at source by means of lower emission limits and more stringent traffic management schemes for vehicles and aircraft. Measures include total bans on lorries during sensitive hours and integrated transport plans for major cities to reduce the use of private cars.

Table 1. **Key attributes of noise abatement policy, case study countries**

AUSTRALIA	National/Local:	Responsibility for noise is split between federal and state authorities. For new motor vehicles, federal law sets noise emission levels determined on the advice of the Advisory Committee on Vehicle Emissions and Noise (ACVEN), a State/Federal environment and transport officials committee. State laws for motor vehicles focus on in-service enforcement. Aircraft noise is controlled by the Federal government. For other sources, the Environmental Noise Control Committee (ENCC) advises the Australian and New Zealand Environment Council (ANZEC) and co-ordinates state policies and actions.
	Main Legislation:	Federal Motor Vehicle Standards Act 1989 Victoria – Environmental Protection Act 1970. W. Australia – Noise Abatement Act 1972-81. Tasmania – Environmental Protection Act 1973. NS Wales – Noise Control Act 1975. South Australia – Noise Control Act 1976-77. Queensland – Noise Abatement Act 1978.
	Key noise issues:	– Motor vehicle noise from new and in-use vehicles (including brakes and tyres). – Land use planning (including noise control in new road building). – Neighbourhood noise from equipment, music, dogs, shooting ranges and intruder alarms. – Works approval and licensing controls for industrial and commercial activities and blasting. – Motor sports and helicopters.
	Use of non-regulatory measures:	– Labelling. – Time and space restrictions. – Public education campaigns. – Sound insulation requirements for new buildings by roads.
	Outstanding uses:	– Stationary noise testing of in-use motor vehicles. – Labelling of low-noise products such as air conditioners, lawn-mowers, chainsaws. – Time and space restrictions for items such as chainsaws, lawn-mowers, hi-fi equipment, televisions. – Public awareness campaigns on driving and neighbourhood noise.

Table 1 *(cont.)*

FRANCE

National/Local: Ministry of Environment, Pollution Prevention Noise Unit has co-ordination powers. National Council on Noise (established 1982) has eight commissions dealing with vehicles, building and urban development, industry, neighbourhood noise, research and communications. Ministry of Transport has a Technical Bureau for Vehicle Emissions. Planning powers are at local level, financial power at national level for raising charges, paying subsidies or compensation.

Main legislation: No framework legislation exists on noise; legal control is mainly through local planning and Road Traffic Code (amended 1969). Aircraft noise charges will require new legislation for a parafiscal tax.

Key noise issues:
  - Control of vehicle noise at source (including tyre/surface noise).
  - Inventory of traffic noise "black spots".
  - Local agreements on noise prevention (noise monitoring, public transport, traffic management, soundproofing).
  - Noise mapping along highways and future TGV railway lines.

Use of non-regulatory measures:
  - Government support for R&D on low noise vehicles.
  - Public information and awareness.
  - Noise barriers and insulation to alleviate "blackspots".

Outstanding uses:
  - Night-time lorry bans through town centres (e.g. Blois).
  - Pilot towns – Department of Environment gave 50 per cent subsidy for a three-year contract for campaigns to reduce noise by traffic management, noise mapping, public awareness, insulation and noise barriers.
  - Zoning 200 m either side of new highways.
  - Virages project/Renault VI R&D project to produce new prototypes.

Table 1   *(cont.)*

GERMANY	National/Local:	Federal Ministry of Environment supported by the Federal Environmental Agency (Umweltbundesamt) is responsible for environmental legislation activities in co-operation with the Federal Ministry of Transport and the Federal Ministry of Labour, but implementation and finance are largely at Länder and municipalities level.
	Main legislation:	Federal law on Protection against Emissions (1974, 1985) relating to traffic and industrial plant. 1968 General Administrative Regulations for installations requiring licensing. 1971 Air Traffic Noise Abatement Act, revised 1977. Road Traffic Ordinance (STVO) 1984, conditions for exempting low-noise vehicles from restrictions.
	Key noise issues:	– Combat noise at source (vehicles, construction equipment, industrial machinery etc.). – Encourage production of low-noise products. – Restrain traffic in sensitive areas. – Prevent noise nuisance through planning. – Noise barriers (up to 1988, more than 1 200 km).
	Use of non-regulatory measures:	– Economic incentives to encourage low-noise products. – Subsidies for R&D of low-noise products. – Environmental labelling. – Environmental traffic management. – Consumer/public education on noise issues.
	Outstanding uses:	– Lorry ban scheme with exemption for low-noise vehicles in Bad Reichenhall. – Subsidies for low-noise vehicles. – Environmental quality labelling e.g. low-noise motorised bicycles, lawn-mowers and construction machinery. – Consideration of vehicle noise in industrial premise licensing. – Research on quiet driving technology and Auto 2 000.

Table 1 *(cont.)*

JAPAN	National/Local:	Environment Agency, established in 1971, is responsible for developing policy, establishing environmental quality standards for noise, setting regulatory standards and enforcing the Noise Regulation Law. The Ministry of Transport is responsible for enforcement of traffic noise laws. Ministry of Construction and local government are responsible for planning and local business noise.
	Main legislation:	Noise Regulation Law 1968, amended 1970, which established Environmental Quality Standards for road traffic, industrial and construction activities in 1971. Law concerning Prevention of Aircraft Noise in the Vicinity of Public Airports, 1973. General Plan for Countermeasures against Shinkansen Railway Noise, 1976.
	Key noise issues:	– Control of road and rail traffic noise at source. – Achievement of Environmental Quality Standards (EQSs) for Noise through zoning. – Alleviating traffic and industrial noise black spots. – Reduction of neighbourhood noise through public education and local by-laws.
	Use of non-regulatory measures:	– Subsidies for R&D for low-noise vehicles in early 1980s. – Reducing noise at source through changes in rail/road/airport design and traffic management. – Compensation for sound insulation to achieve EQSs. – Noise barriers. – Public awareness.
	Outstanding uses:	– Promotion of suitable land uses around roads and Shinkansen railways (including banks, trees, noise barriers, non-sensitive buildings). – Relocation of noisy industrial facilities from residential areas if noise abatement technology is not considered economic. – Widespread use of noise barriers along highways and railways. – Compensation from Airport Authorities and National Railways Corporation for relocation or insulation of dwellings. – "Quiet communities" to raise awareness and eliminate neighbourhood noise on a pilot town basis.

Table 1 *(cont.)*

THE NETHERLANDS	National/Local:	Ministry of Housing, Physical Planning and Environment oversees in consultation with the Ministries of Transport and Waterways.
	Main legislation:	Noise Nuisance Act 1979 covers noise at source from equipment, industry, traffic, entertainment/recreation, military airports, and provides for grants, R&D funds, charges, etc. Aviation Act - aircraft noise. Working Conditions Act - protection of workers against noise.
	Key noise issues:	– Lowering emission levels at source (traffic). – Elimination of "blackspots" (industrial, traffic, railway and aircraft noise). – Quiet zones. – Zoning around noise-generating sites and alongside roads and railways. – Financial subsidies for low-noise technologies.
	Use of non-regulatory measures:	– Traffic management schemes. – Financial subsidies for insulation and noise screening. – Government support for R&D.
	Outstanding uses:	– Subsidies for super-quiet heavy goods vehicles (HGV). – Fuel charge. – Low-noise purchasing policies. – Zoning around railways, industrial sites, roads and airports and compensation for insulation. – Quiet zones in nature areas.

Table 1 *(cont.)*

SWITZERLAND	National/Local:	Ministry of the Environment, Noise Abatement Unit. Co-ordination between Departments of Planning and Transport at municipal and local level to implement traffic management schemes.
	Main legislation:	Federal Environmental Protection Act, 1985, is the major framework legislation. Federal Ordinance on Protection Against Noise, 1986, sets maximum permissible ambient noise levels and new building regulations. Federal Ordinance on Construction of Vehicles, 1969, sets vehicle emission limits.
	Key noise issues:	– Tight source emission standards to achieve the best practicable noise abatement technology. – Control of building in noisy areas. – Environmental traffic management incorporated in planning. – Public awareness. – Soundproofing.
	Use of non-regulatory measures:	– Speed limits. – Bans on heavy goods vehicles (HGV) at night-time and weekends. – Driver awareness campaigns. – Time and space restrictions.
	Outstanding uses:	– Restrictions on operation of noisy equipment, lawnmowers, etc., and lorries at night-time in noise-sensitive areas. – Zurich environmental traffic management scheme providing for expansion of public transport, speed limits and traffic flow controls. – Recommendations for sound insulation requirements in new buildings.

Source: OECD.

Chapter 2

ROAD TRAFFIC NOISE

1. INTRODUCTION

Ambient noise levels

A variety of studies and surveys carried out in OECD countries indicate that road traffic noise is a major source of disamenity and that between 32 per cent and 80 per cent of the population were exposed to road traffic noise above 55 dB(A) in the early 1980s[3]. At levels of noise above 65 dB(A) constrained behaviour patterns consistent with serious damage occur; in all of the case study countries, significant numbers of the population experience these levels of nuisance.

Sources of traffic noise

Traffic noise arises directly from the vehicle (e.g. engine, exhaust outlet, vibration) and also from the interface between the tyres and the road surface and the way the vehicle is driven. Since heavy trucks and buses are the major cause of noise, these have taken precedence in policy–making; cars and motorcycles are an important source of noise because of their growing numbers, but noise is substantially a result of how they are driven and maintained (especially exhaust), and policies concerning them have a slightly different focus.

Noise transmission (and ultimately the extent of nuisance) depends on the distance between the source and the receiver and on intervening screens and reflective surfaces. The ambient noise levels depend on the position and sound insulation of buildings.

The major problem facing OECD countries is that despite policies to control noise emissions from individual vehicles, ambient noise levels, and thus nuisance, are expected to increase over time because of the following factors:

— The increased number of sources (i.e. increased traffic on the road);
— Increased mobility in terms of distance travelled and extended hours and areas of operation;
— Longer life of heavy vehicles; in Japan, for instance, where noise regulations on new vehicles are taking a long time to have a bearing on the existing fleet, the government is trying to reverse this trend by introducing tax benefits for new vehicles;
— The increased exposure of the population to traffic noise because of building programmes and pressure on development space in city centres.

Figure 1. **MEASURES TO REDUCE VEHICLE NOISE POLLUTION**

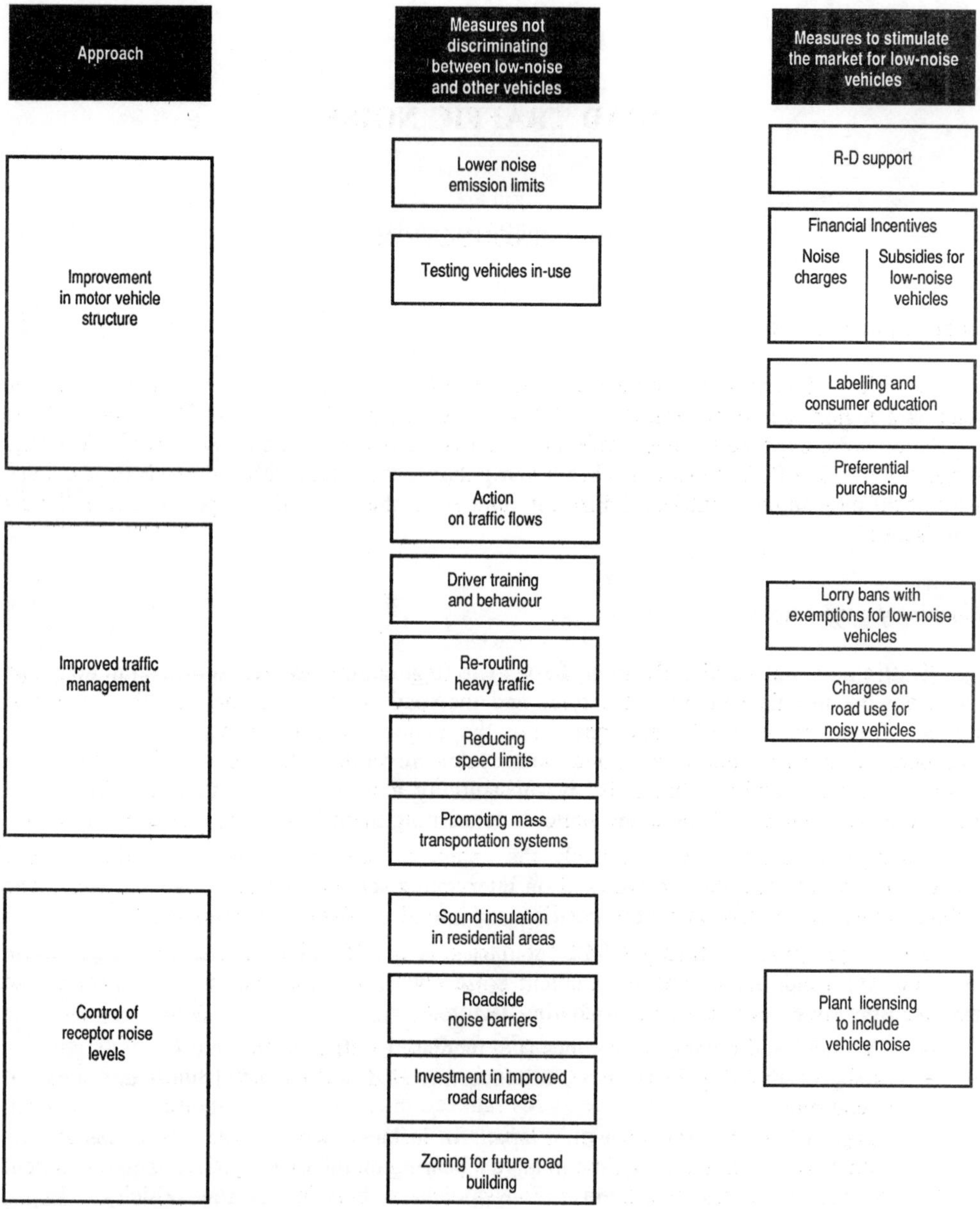

Approach	Measures not discriminating between low-noise and other vehicles	Measures to stimulate the market for low-noise vehicles
Improvement in motor vehicle structure	Lower noise emission limits	R-D support
	Testing vehicles in-use	Financial Incentives / Noise charges / Subsidies for low-noise vehicles
		Labelling and consumer education
		Preferential purchasing
Improved traffic management	Action on traffic flows	Lorry bans with exemptions for low-noise vehicles
	Driver training and behaviour	Charges on road use for noisy vehicles
	Re-routing heavy traffic	
	Reducing speed limits	
	Promoting mass transportation systems	
Control of receptor noise levels	Sound insulation in residential areas	Plant licensing to include vehicle noise
	Roadside noise barriers	
	Investment in improved road surfaces	
	Zoning for future road building	

Source: OECD.

Measures for reducing traffic noise

Since commercial vehicles on average emit between 7 and 12 dB(A) higher noise levels than passenger vehicles (implying that one lorry produces approximately the same sound pressure as 5 to 15 cars), policy in OECD countries has focused on reducing lorry noise at source. This has been attempted principally through regulations on maximum vehicle noise emissions. Emission limits are being supplemented by a range of supporting policies (Figure 1). They concern:

1. Reduction of noise at source through:
   — Emission limits for motor vehicles;
   — Improvement of vehicle design to reduce noise emissions;
   — Financial incentives for production and use of low–noise vehicles;
   — Labelling and consumer education to encourage use of low–noise vehicles and low–noise driving patterns.
2. Reduction of noise transmission through improved traffic management:
   — Environmental traffic management, (e.g. reduced speed limits, continuous traffic flows);
   — Time and space restrictions on noisy vehicles;
   — Change of modal split (e.g. improved public transport, use of bicycles);
   — Information and education.
3. Control of receptor noise levels through non–vehicular measures (i.e. measures which reduce noise at source but are not within the scope of action of the vehicle manufacturer or operator):
   — Land use planning;
   — Roadside noise barriers;
   — Insulation in residential areas;
   — Investment in improved road surfaces.

The following sections describe how effective various measures have proved in practice.

2. NOISE EMISSION LIMITS

Emission limits for new vehicles

In all OECD countries noise emission regulations for new vehicles have been an important noise abatement policy (Table 2). The most widely employed standards are those using the ISO R362 test procedure, whose objective is to reproduce the highest noise levels which can be expected under urban driving conditions. This procedure has been adopted by both the European Community (EC) and the United Nations' Economic Commission for Europe (ECE); the technical directives for both Organisations are broadly similar. The limits laid down in EC regulations during the 1970s reduced individual vehicle noise by 2–3 dB(A) and will reduce levels by at least 4 dB(A) once the 84/424/EEC limits have been adopted.

However, in Japan and Switzerland, regulations have evolved more rapidly. In most OECD countries, governments are party to supranational or federal regulations; as a result, governments such as those of Germany and the Netherlands, which would like to tighten emission limits in their respective countries, are severely hindered.

Table 2. **Vehicle noise emission limits in selected countries, dB(A), (ISO R362 - 1964)[1]**

Vehicle weight(t) power (kw)	Heavy lorries			Small commercial vehicles		Buses		Cars	Motor-cycles
	>3.5 >150	75-100	<75	2.0-3.5	<2.0	Large >150	Small <150		
Australia									
Current: [2, 3]	89	87	87	82	82	88	86	81	80
Future: [2, 4]	84	83	81	79	78	83	80	77	80
Japan	83		83	78		83[5]	83[5]	78	75
Switzerland	84	82	80	77		82	80	75	73-86[6]
EC									
Current:	88	86		81		85	82	80	82
Future:	84[7]	83[7]	81[7]	79[8]	78[8]	83[8]	80[8]	77[9]	80[10]

1. Type testing by a drive-by test using a microphone at a height of 1.2 m and a distance of 7.5 m from the centre line of the vehicle.
2. Limits for close proximity exhaust noise also apply.
3. Subtracts 1 dB(A) for equivalence with EC limits (except motorcycles).
4. Standards consistent with 84/424/EEC from 1992/93.
5. With more than 11 passengers.
6. All motorcycle measures in second gear.
7. 84/424/EEC limits from 1st October 1990.
8. 84/424/EEC limits from 1st October 1989 – diesel engines had until 1st October 1990 to comply.
9. 84/424/EEC limits from 1st October 1988 for new type approvals.
10. 78/1 015/EEC and 87/56. Stage 2 limits from 1995/96.

Source: OECD.

64

The Dutch proposals for the new standards in the medium term (by the year 2000) and long term (by the year 2015) are considerably lower than current limits. In the medium term, levels of 74 dB(A) for passenger cars and 74–76 dB(A) for heavy vehicles are envisaged; by 2015 these would be reduced to 70 dB(A) for cars and 75 dB(A) for lorries. Only in Switzerland is national legislation based on the principle of the best practicable noise abatement technology. Switzerland, therefore, has significantly more stringent regulations than the EC or ECE for all vehicles but has experienced some difficulties in encouraging local production of heavy vehicles because the additional costs in using the best available technology could not be supported by such a small domestic market. Heavy vehicles are currently supplied by German, Dutch and Scandinavian manufacturers from their low–noise range of vehicles with modified engines and part encapsulation. The premium costs for low–noise vehicles are borne by the users.

In many OECD countries, governments have sponsored research and development (R&D) intended to identify technical possibilities and help national manufacturers gear up production in order to meet future legislative requirements. These programmes have been largely completed and have been successful in achieving their stated objectives of:

— Researching engine design and layout modifications;
— Producing low–noise prototypes;
— Testing prototypes in use over longer periods to assess technical and economic feasibility.

New limits have been agreed and set, with systematic reduction over the years. Maximum noise levels are set for prototypes, and government agencies carry out tests on selected vehicles from the production line.

In Australia, there has been considerable discussion, and the introduction of EC or ECE noise emission limits has been delayed for most vehicle categories. Limits consistent with 78/1015/EEC for motorcycles were implemented in 1988, but limits consistent with 84/424/EEC for other vehicle categories will not apply until 1992/93. Australian requirements also include compliance with close proximity exhaust noise limits.

International standards are generally low in comparison to technical possibilities, but the ability of governments to request that vehicles meet more stringent requirements is limited by the legal framework; this varies between countries, and is not entirely clear. For instance, in the United Kingdom, the municipalities have interpreted EC regulations as permitting local authorities or Member states to impose emission limits for noise sources not covered by the drive–by test. This has been applied in London, where lorries with exhaust silencers, quietened airbrakes and bodywork (modified to prevent low frequency vibrations) may be exempted from night–time driving bans which apply to vehicles merely meeting EC regulations (Inset 1).

In Germany, the legal framework allows for a more radical approach. Germany has been the leader in establishing an absolute definition of "low–noise" vehicles (Table 2, above). The noise emission limits are up to 5 dB(A) quieter than the EC directives which took effect in 1988/89. The German legal definition has been adopted in Austria, is under consideration in Norway, and is used as the basis for introducing incentives for the purchase of low–noise vehicles (Inset 4).

Given the long time–lag involved, both in reducing limits and in their having an effect on the existing fleet of vehicles (since vehicles may be used for 10–12 years), introducing emission limits for in–use vehicles may be one effective approach.

Inset 1

Noise emission limits: EC directives

Since 1970, through a series of directives, the European Community has set maximum permissible noise emission levels for motor vehicles, including private and commercial passenger vehicles, heavy goods vehicles, motorcycles and tractors[1]. The limits have been continuously lowered but the major provisions remain unchanged, namely:

— *Each type produced must receive a type approval certificate which includes noise pressure level tests;*
— *If the directives are adopted by a Member State, vehicles may be marketed only if they meet the limits;*
— *They may not be refused entry to any country if they* do *meet these limits;*
— *There is a transition period between the date when new type approvals must meet the limits and the date when the limits become mandatory for all vehicles registered;*
— *Member States are expected to make these provisions mandatory in line with the single market.*

All the directives have been transposed by Member States into their national legislation and all EC manufacturers are meeting current emission levels or, in the case of motorcycles, working towards future limits.

In practice, the directives have become mandatory at different rates in different countries. In particular, three approaches may be distinguished:

— *Those countries most concerned with road traffic noise have automatically adopted directives at the first permissible dates and made them mandatory (France, Germany, the Netherlands and the United Kingdom);*
— *Countries with no domestic manufacturers and no national type approval system adopted directives straight away (Denmark, Greece and Portugal) but either rely on type approval certificates from other countries, or do not intend to make limits mandatory unless pressed to at some future date (Ireland and Luxembourg);*
— *Countries such as Belgium, Italy and Spain have adopted the directives as mandatory but have taken advantage of the transitional arrangements and will apply them with some time lag.*

Those countries, where the directives are mandatory, set maximum limits which apply equally to EC manufacturers and imported vehicles and may refuse entry to vehicles which do not have EC type approval. In Ireland and Luxembourg, however, any vehicle which meets any other Member State's national type approval cannot be refused entry. There are several examples of manufacturers of Japanese and southeast Asian cars,

---

1. Motor vehicles directives on admissible noise from engines and exhaust systems. 70/157/EEC, 73/350/EEC, 77/212/EEC, 81/334/EEC, 84/372/EEC, 84/424/EEC.
   Motorcycles: 78/1015/EEC, 87/56/EEC, 89/235/EEC.
   Tractors: 74/151/EEC (exterior noise), 77/311/EEC drivers in–cab noise.

Inset 1 *(cont.)*

Noise emission limits: EC directives

which would not meet the EC standards already in force in France, Germany, the Netherlands and the United Kingdom, using the Irish market for product launching, in the hope that they will then gain access to other EC markets.

For those countries, such as Germany and the Netherlands, which would like to impose more stringent limits, the regulatory possibilities are considerably narrowed, for the directives specify that no vehicle that meets EC limits may be refused entry and this effectively rules out tighter national limits on the grounds that they would constitute trade restrictions. The only options to overcome this are: 1) to legally define quieter vehicles, 2) to apply economic instruments so as to encourage their widespread use, and/or 3) to introduce limits on the use of noisier vehicles at certain times in certain places. The latter approach was announced in by Austria, which intends to place a night–time ban on all lorry movements, except those of low–noise vehicles. No EC manufacturer had a standard production vehicle which would meet this definition by Autumn 1989 and EC manufacturers considered this move a restrictive practice.

The directives have aimed to achieve state–of–the–art noise emission levels within the context of economic and market limits. Accordingly, there has generally been a span of up to five years between the announcement of the directive and the date of compliance, allowing manufacturers ample time to meet standards through both collaborative and independent research. Manufacturers' associations and manufacturers themselves, however, have expressed some concern over future reductions in limits:

a) *Goods vehicles*

   The 84/424 limits became effective from October 1989 and were to be implemented across the entire range by October 1990. There have been no technical problems in meeting these standards, which has been achieved through engine modifications and changes in body design; no encapsulation has been necessary. However, manufacturers felt that before establishing further goals, which might emerge as a result of a more recent EC working party, the following points should be taken into consideration:

   — *Regulations could not go further without assessing the situation;*
   — *Between two and five years were needed to consider the environmental impact and technical difficulties as a result of 84/424;*
   — *Current regulations require that* all *vehicles meet the limits (as opposed to ECE regulations that only require compliance* on the average). *This means production models must be designed to −2 dB(A) below the limits to allow for production tolerances;*
   — *Clarification is needed of test procedures, since variations of up to 8 dB(A) can be achieved by varying some aspect of the conditions (instruments, road surface, tyres or atmospheric conditions) marginally;*

Inset 1 *(cont.)*

Noise emission limits: EC directives

— *With more stringent noise emission levels (as in Swiss regulations) the tyre–road surface noise becomes an increasingly important component of rolling noise. But it is beyond the manufacturers' control.*

b) **Cars**

The 84/424 limits both for new type approvals and for all models are already effective in many countries. No technical problems have been experienced with the 77 dB(A) limits, but manufacturers currently find Swiss limits of 75 dB(A) difficult to meet and are able to offer only a limited range of automatic transmission models for this market. Doubts have been expressed about future reductions in EC limits:

— *Below 80 dB(A) some 95 per cent of rolling noise is attributable to tyre–road interface; car manufacturers can only work on the remaining 5 per cent and they feel the Dutch targets are too optimistic unless there is a breakthrough in tyre and road surface technology;*

— *German manufacturers are the only ones who have included noise levels in their vehicle documentation; there is no evidence that consumers are interested in car noise, and manufacturers feel that reduction of gaseous and particulate emissions is a greater priority.*

c) **Motorcycles**

The Stage I limits of 77–82 dB(A) are in effect in all countries except Portugal. Manufacturers are working towards Stage II limits by October 1995 for motorcycles of less than 80 cc and over 175 cc, and by the following year for middle range motorcycles. The views expressed by manufacturers about future limits may be summarised as follows:

— *For large motorcycles, 80 dB(A) is state–of–the–art with current test procedures; below this, engine encapsulation will be required;*

— *Attention should be turned to testing and limiting noise levels of vehicles in use; this is considered the only way to reduce motorcycle noise nuisance since much of the noise comes from badly maintained, or badly tuned, motorcycles;*

— *Manufacturers test and label parts, particularly exhaust silencers, but in–use motorcycles are often modified, a practice which may increase noise levels by 10 dB(A); all components should be type–approved and owners of illegally modified vehicles should be fined.*

d) **Tractors**

The directives for external tractor noise levels were introduced in 1974 and have been applied since the early 1980s. They require improvements to exhaust systems and radiator fans, but manufacturers are now producing vehicles as quiet as

Testing vehicles in use

In Japan, in–use motor vehicles are required to undergo periodic noise inspections and tests to make sure that they continue to meet the regulations for vehicles which applied when they were new and that they do not deteriorate over time. In some Australian states, vehicles are subject to on–road "spotting" and subsequent testing to enforce the "close proximity" exhaust noise limit (Inset 2).

In Japan, in–use motor vehicles are periodically noise tested in the street to make sure they are well–maintained. Measurement has become more convenient recently, with the introduction of a proximity test, whereas previous roadside tests were cumbersome, requiring measurement at 20 metre from the exhaust. Proximity tests were introduced in 1986 for motorcycles, in 1988 for cars and in 1989 for lorries.

In Germany and the Netherlands, vehicle checks are carried out on a regular basis but do not include noise tests; they do, however, involve checking that exhaust silencers are intact. An in–situ motorcycle test has been developed based on engine size but is not yet widely used.

3.   ECONOMIC INCENTIVES FOR LOW–NOISE VEHICLES

In several countries governments have taken steps to encourage the use of vehicles quieter than required by regulations, in order to create a market for low–noise vehicles before more stringent international regulations are introduced. Approaches to creating both a supply of and a demand for low–noise vehicles have included:

— Subsidies for incremental capital costs;
— Grants for R&D;
— Preferential purchasing policies;
— Charges on noisy vehicles.

Inset 2

In–use noise testing: Australia

In Australia, surveys indicate that over 17 per cent of the population identify noise from vehicles as a major nuisance. In order to combat this nuisance, some states have introduced simple, close–proximity exhaust noise tests, which can be carried out at the roadside or in testing centres. Vehicles that do not comply with prescribed limits[1] may be subject to legal penalty. According to surveys, 2–3 per cent of all vehicles on the road would exceed the limits. Non–compliance for heavy vehicles is estimated at 5–8 per cent and for motorcycles at 25 per cent. The main reasons for non–compliance are modified or inappropriately specified exhaust system components. Repairs following test failure usually cost in the range A\$10–400 (US\$11–450) for cars, up to A\$50–1 200 (US\$55–1 350) for heavy vehicles. Resources available for testing and enforcement programmes are severely limited. Nevertheless, effectiveness is claimed to be high. The different states apply somewhat differing approaches, requiring varying degrees of co–operation between environment agencies, police and registration authorities.

In Adelaide, South Australia, enforcement of vehicle noise requirements is primarily the responsibility of the Department of Transport (DOT), with policy advice from the Department of Environment and Planning. Police officers encountering vehicles on the road which have safety or noise defects serve the owner a "defect notice" which must be cleared by undergoing a full safety and noise check at a DOT–operated Inspection Station. If vehicles fail this check, their registrations are cancelled pending satisfactory repairs. The programme works well, and since noise aspects are built into a programme set up for safety reasons, the incremental costs for noise control are small. (Currently, only cars and motorcycles are subject to noise testing, as South Australian requirements do not yet include the close–proximity procedure and limits for heavy vehicles.)

---

1. The close–proximity exhaust noise test and limits applied in Australia are as follows:

   Motor cars: Microphone at 0.5 metre from the exhaust outlet with engine at 75 per cent engine speed at maximum power (ESMP).
   Limits applied:
   — for cars manufactured before 1/1/83: 96 dB(A)
   — for cars manufactured after 1/1/83: 90 dB(A).

   Motorcycles: Microphone at 0.5 metre from the exhaust outlet with engine at 50 per cent ESMP, then back–off (as in the stationary test specified in 78/1015 EEC).
   Limits applied:
   — for M/CS manufactured before 1/3/85: 100 dB(A)
   — for M/CS manufactured after 1/3/85: 94 dB(A).

   Diesel lorries and buses: Microphone at 1.0 metre from the exhaust outlet. Engine is accelerated from low idle to maximum speed and then returned to idle. Noise level is maximum recorded.
   Limits applied:
   — Differ according to Gross Vehicle Mass and year of manufacture.
   — For vehicles manufactured after 1/7/83 the limits range from 95 dB(A) (less than 3 500 kg) up to 99 dB(A) (greater than 12 000 kg) — (Add 4 dB(A) for vertical exhaust system).

Inset 2 *(cont.)*

In–use noise testing: Australia

In New South Wales, the State Pollution Control Commission (SPCC) is responsible for vehicle noise enforcement and conducts routine road patrols. Noisy vehicles may be stopped (where it is safe to do so) and tested at the roadside, and offenders may be prosecuted. Owners whose vehicles could not be stopped are contacted through their registration numbers and served an inspection notice requiring them to present their vehicles for test at an SPCC–operated site. Sufficient time is given for owners to effect repairs, so only a small proportion of vehicles fail. If vehicles fail, their registrations are suspended pending satisfactory repairs. Random roadside testing is also carried out on a campaign basis, for heavy vehicles. Some thousands of vehicles are subject to such actions each year and average noise reductions of 9 dB(A) are achieved. The SPCC in conjunction with the New South Wales Roads and Traffic Authority (RTA) is planning to introduce noise testing for heavy vehicles subject to random on–road safety inspection by the RTA. This is a very large statewide programme which, once noise testing is incorporated, would quickly bring the heavy vehicle fleet into almost total compliance with the law. A pilot study has shown that incremental costs for noise enforcement would be quite small. The SPCC and RTA are also examining the possibility of adopting noise tests in annual registration inspections for cars and motorcycles. This, however, would be problematic as testing is carried out by a large number of privately owned garages, which currently do not have acoustic testing equipment.

In Victoria, the Environment Protection Authority (EPA) has responsibility for vehicle noise enforcement, and has developed its programmes similarly to New South Wales. The EPA has developed very close co–operation with police, who do most on the on–road spotting.

The EPA has also authorised a number of private exhaust specialists to conduct tests on vehicles "defected" by police. Defect notices are then cleared by the EPA on presentation of a test certificate. To obtain EPA authorisation, exhaust specialists must have the necessary equipment, costing approximately A$3 600 (US$4 050), and must pass a training session. The test costs the summoned driver A$13 (US$14.50), which is paid to the authorised tester. A fine of up to A$500 may apply for owners who do not clear defect notices. In addition to the above, owners whose vehicles are defected may be served infringement notices with a penalty of A$100 (US$112).

The EPA programme has proved to be very effective; it is well regarded by the police, who are highly co–operative in its implementation, and is well supported by the public and the automotive trades.

These Australian programmes depend on the use of the close–proximity exhaust noise test with appropriately specified limits. This simply and effectively discriminates between noisy and non–noisy exhaust systems. The programmes appear to be much better supported by police and the public, than the more subjective programmes used to less effect in some other countries. The Australian programmes are not expensive to operate and appear easy to implement within the context of international regulations for new vehicles.

Experience with these measures is described in the following paragraphs. To make the use of any economic incentives for low–noise vehicles feasible, it has been important to define exactly what is meant by "low–noise". In Germany, a regulatory definition has been developed[4] and used to enable a range of measures, e.g. labelling low–noise vehicles; it has since been adopted in Austria. In the Netherlands, a relative, rather than an absolute criterion, for subsidising low–noise vehicles is in use (Inset 3). This has proved a useful approach for dealing with changing circumstances so that operators qualify for a "maximum and minimum" subsidy where their vehicles are quieter than legal limits by 6 dB(A) and 3 dB(A), respectively. This definition has accommodated changing means of measuring emission limits and the increasing ability of manufacturers to produce low–noise vehicles[5] (Table 3).

Table 3. **Definitions of low-noise vehicles**

Weight	>3.5t	Heavy Lorries	
Power	>150	75 - 150	<75
EC Current	88	86	86
Germany[a]	80	78	77
Netherlands[b]	–	79	–

a) Low-noise vehicle definition over 2.8 tonnes, Road Transport Licensing Ordinance, Annex XXI, November 1984. Includes driving, engine, brake and omni-directional noise.
b) Over 12 tonnes.
Source: OECD.

Subsidies for capital costs

Contacts with manufacturers suggest that low–noise technology may increase capital costs of vehicles by between 2–10 per cent of the purchase price[6]. One approach to this problem which is used in the Netherlands and parts of Germany is that of compensatory subsidies. The aim of such a scheme is to provide a stimulus to both vehicle operators and manufacturers to use and produce low–noise vehicles, thus creating a self–sustaining market. Operators receive the additional capital costs of buying low–noise vehicles through tax allowances or grants. In addition, subsidies to vehicle operators indirectly subsidise manufacturers, in that the manufacturers are able to spread some of the development overheads over a larger number of units than they would have sold ordinarily. The necessary conditions for a subsidy scheme, judging from the Dutch experience, are the following:

— A realistic legal definition of "low–noise" vehicles which meet the criteria for financial assistance;

Inset 3

Subsidies and charges to encourage use of low–noise vehicles: the Netherlands

The Netherlands introduced a dual financial approach to encouraging low–noise vehicles: on the one hand, offering environmental investment premiums for investments which reduce noise levels below legal requirements; on the other hand, introducing a system for charging the owners of noisy vehicles according to the potential noise nuisance of their emissions. In the case of lorries, charges were to be steeply progressive and would double for every 3 dB(A) of noise. Charges, based on the potential noise nuisance emitted, have never been directly implemented; instead, subsidies have become the focus of policy and a general fuel charge was implemented.

From 1981 the Ministry of Housing, Physical Planning and Environment has implemented a two–tier subsidy according to the level of noise reductions achieved below the EC standards. This system has changed with time. Originally, maximum and minimum subsidy levels were 7.5 per cent and 3 per cent for reductions of 6 dB(A) and 3 dB(A), respectively. In 1988, because of reduced availability of funds, only heavy lorries (over 12 tonnes) with emissions of 79 dB(A) or less were eligible, receiving a maximum subsidy of 4.5 per cent. According to industry sources, there is discussion about increasing subsidies to 5 per cent and defining eligible vehicles as "super–quiet". The concept of a "super–quiet" vehicle, with associated labelling provisions, has been accepted by administrators but still requires debate and agreement in Parliament. Local authorities will be asked to use this definition to frame preferential purchasing policies.

According to evaluations carried out in 1988, the scheme, which was part of a larger investment subsidy programme, was very successful. Nonetheless, it was abolished for general budget reasons. In the period 1 January 1988 until 1990, Gld 6.75 million still remained available for compensatory grants for low–noise trucks. Plans for 1990–2010 include a new subsidy programme for low–noise and clean lorries and buses to an amount of Gld 90 million.

	Percentage of lorries and buses receiving minimum subsidy (reduction of 3 dB(A)), 1981–87						
	1981	1982	1983	1984	1985	1986	1987
Light lorry (3.5–12 t)	60	88	85	30[a]	60	74	—
Heavy lorry (>12 t)	75	78	96	45[a]	28	2 580[b]	
No. of applications[c]	550	3 610	4 534	5 510	6 524	7 848	6 200[b]
Estimated premium (?)							
— Gld million	3.8	20.2	27.9	30.3	32.2	62.7	17.6[d]
— US$	1.8	9.5	13.2	14.3	15.2	29.6	8.3

a) By 1984, the majority of lorries were well below the limit; accordingly, thresholds for awarding grants were changed.
b) Ministry estimates.
c) An application may cover more than one vehicle.
d) Six months.
Source: Ministry of Housing, Physical Planning and Environment, various years.

— The availability of funds to finance a potentially open–ended scheme, although schemes should become systematically less costly as the vehicle fleet is renewed and could, in theory, be cross–subsidised by charges on noisy vehicles;

— Co–operation of vehicle manufacturers in developing low–noise vehicles for small markets;

— Availability of low–noise vehicles[7].

Subsidy schemes are operated in the Netherlands (Inset 3, above) and two towns in Germany, Bad Reichenhall (Inset 4) and Berlin. The German schemes allow a subsidy to the buyer of the vehicle of up to DM 2 000 (US$1 200) for vehicles defined as low–noise (Table 3, above). A manufacturer's certificate of prototype approval is sufficient proof that the vehicle meets this standard but, in Bad Reichenhall, operators must also be prepared to advertise that they are using low–noise trucks, buses or diesel taxis with noise labels visibly displayed on the side of the vehicle.

Where subsidies have been available, maximum levels of co–operation are received from manufacturers, for whom the subsidies are a stimulus to introduce noise abatement measures into their standard production models. Elsewhere, however, such co–operation has not materialised because producing low–noise vehicles entails retooling costs and, without guaranteed markets, domestic manufacturers are not prepared to carry those costs alone.

Grants for research and development (R&D)

Direct support by government for R&D into low–noise vehicles is an instrument which can act directly as an incentive as it reduces the costs of developing quiet products.

Very few R&D programmes have been entirely funded by government; in France, Renault Véhicules Industriels (RVI) funded three quarters of the Virages project[8] and, in Japan, MITI[9] provided loans, rather than grants, to four manufacturers in a research programme in order to assist them in meeting more stringent regulations. In Australia, a central government tax incentive scheme allows 150 per cent tax deductions against any approved R&D costing more than A$50 000 (US$56 300) for a range of vehicle innovations. This was introduced for a limited period to stimulate Australian R&D and will be phased out over future years. No manufacturer has yet taken up the scheme for noise control research.

The majority of programmes were carried out in the late 1970s and, having achieved their objectives of developing technologies and low–noise prototypes and testing them in–use, were completed and wound up in the mid–1980s. Several of the case study countries, however, still have ongoing programmes. These include the "Auto 2000" research programme in Germany, funded by the Ministry of Research and Technology, for the purpose of developing and testing prototypes with several improved features. The programme intends to produce vehicles for operation by 2000 with emissions of only 73 dB(A).

A second phase of the French Virages project started in 1988; the first stage had identified noise abatement techniques which have not been incorporated in mass production types because the market is not sufficiently developed to justify the additional costs. The focus of R&D in the second phase will be fuel consumption, adiabatic engines and safety.

A common lesson of R&D programmes appears to be that manufacturers take little interest in the noise issue in the absence of either consumer demand or more stringent emission regulations anticipated in the future. In order to encourage further engine research a market must exist as a result of other economic incentives; these may be subsidies or

Inset 4

Lorry bans: model — Bad Reichenhall, Germany

In 1981 the town of Bad Reichenhall introduced a policy which created incentives for the use of low–noise lorries within the town. Low–noise lorries (as defined in the Road Transport Licensing Ordinance) are exempted from the ban on heavy vehicles which has been in force since 1954, because low–noise vehicles are no noisier than ordinary cars. Low–noise lorries are exempted from traffic restrictions which have been in force since 1954, provided they meet the low–noise lorry definition as described in Annex XXI of the Road Transport Licensing Order.

The restrictions for commercial vehicles, in force since 1954, are as follows:

Pedestrian Zone	*All day, limited exemptions*
Health Resort Area (Zone I)	*All day, limited exemptions*
Shopping Centre (Zone II)	*19.00–07.00*

Under the 1981 rules, it has been possible to obtain wider exemptions for low–noise vehicles. Noisy lorries may be granted short–term permits to enter the zone in return for payment of a fee. This creates an economic incentive to acquire low–noise vehicles.

MAN, Magirus Deutz and Daimler–Benz have co–operated to develop prototypes and production models which meet the low–noise definition. Once vehicles have gained type approval, manufacturers are encouraged to describe vehicles as "lärmarmes Kraftfahrzeug" and to use this as a selling point in sales literature. Daimler–Benz have developed eleven models of 3.2–24 tonnes; MAN have five models between 6–10 tonnes and Magirus have two models of 17 and 24 tonnes on the market. The average increase in price above the standard range is DM 4 500 (US$2 600) equivalent to 3.5–7.0 per cent of capital costs, depending on the model.

So far the increase in capital cost involved for operators has discouraged a large market for low–noise vehicles, although 25 low–noise vehicles are reported to be operating in and around Bad Reichenhall. In April 1988, in order to provide an additional stimulus, the town of Bad Reichenhall decided to offer financial incentives to those prepared to buy low–noise vehicles: a non–repayable subsidy equal to the additional costs for low–noise equipment of up to DM 2 000 (US$1 200) for a lorry and DM 100 (US$60) for a motorised bicycle.

The conditions for the subsidy schemes include the following:

— *The subsidy is dependent on funds available, i.e. it is not a right;*
— *The vehicle should be used by commercial enterprises operating predominantly in Bad Reichenhall;*
— *Stickers indicating that vehicles are low–noise should be visibly displayed.*

The town authorities hope that this promotion programme will serve to increase public awareness, encourage operators to buy low–noise vehicles and stimulate manufacturers to produce more low–noise models. No assessment has yet been made of the effects of the programme.

purchasing policies or may take other forms. For instance, in–cab noise has been reduced as a result of engine modifications and is seen as a strong selling point.

Vehicle noise research is now focusing on tyre and road surface qualities or driver behaviour: (see below).

Preferential purchasing policies

Another approach to creating a market for low–noise vehicles is to encourage major consumers to develop an awareness of noise as a purchasing criterion. This is easiest in the public sector, particularly for public transport and urban service operators.

Few examples exist in the private sector, although CAB[10], in the Netherlands, has become concerned about noise levels for two main reasons: external noise affects the whole community, since buses are forced to operate in residential areas at anti–social times; internal noise is disturbing to both passengers and the driver. The noise goals set by the central association for its 300 new buses each year have been dramatically reduced since 1987; targets of 72 dB(A) for internal noise and 75 dB(A) for external noise are 10 dB(A) below current EC regulations and 4 dB(A) below previous CAB criteria. Prototypes have been developed in close co–operation with Dutch manufacturers; low–noise models, which also incorporate other improved features, are expected to cost Gld 1 500 (US$710) more, or 5 per cent more, than standard models.

In France, the pilot town operators had intended to buy low–noise public service vehicles and the Post Office tested three experimental vehicles with noise levels below 80 dB(A), but these have been abandoned.

In the absence of a government directive, it is necessary for other incentives to exist, such as the subsidies available in the Netherlands until 1988 for a wide range of low–noise vehicles (Inset 3, above) or subsidies available in Bad Reichenhall (Inset 4, above) and Berlin in Germany.

In Germany, the acquisition officers for vehicles and equipment have been instructed to take account of environmental aspects when establishing purchasing criteria[11], where funds permit. This implies that vehicles should meet the "low–noise" definition (Table 3, above).

Exemptions both from bans on night–time lorry operations and from night–time restrictions on vehicle movements on industrial premises have also been used as an incentive to develop low–noise purchasing criteria in Germany. In the absence of financial incentives, operators must perceive a substantial public relations gain from using low–noise vehicles; this has been recognised in Bad Reichenhall where vehicle operators, manufacturers and the scheme's operators mutually benefit from increasing public awareness by labelling vehicles as low–noise.

Noise charges for vehicles

An alternative or complementary policy is to charge "noisy" vehicles or those which do not meet "low–noise" criteria. There is little experience of this in OECD countries, despite the relative success of aircraft noise charges. The Netherlands operated an indirect noise charge for heavy vehicles through levying additional taxes on fuel; equivalent to a surtax of 1.2 per cent of diesel costs in 1986, it amounted to US$19 million. This levy was based on the rationale that old, and therefore probably noisy, vehicles used more fuel and would therefore bear the brunt of fuel taxes. Thus, it was actually linked not with noise output, but with the level of use.

Levying higher taxes for noisy vehicles has also been considered in other countries; it would in theory be possible, for instance, to tax non–"low–noise" vehicles for operation where lorry ban schemes exist. For instance, in Austria, Germany and the United Kingdom, this could cross–finance subsidies to operators buying "low–noise" vehicles. But it has not yet been attempted, partly because legal difficulties are anticipated.

Where in–use vehicles are noise–tested (e.g. Australia and Japan), it would also be possible to levy an annual discretionary noise tax as part of the road registration tax to make sure old vehicles were properly maintained. This could be applied in conjunction with a sliding scale tax for noisier types of new vehicles and would have an incentive effect on manufacturers, since the noisier vehicles would be more costly for their customers to run.

Road–pricing schemes being discussed in the Netherlands include attempts to include a charge to cover the annual mileage travelled and the area of operation (i.e. urban or rural). These are not directly noise–related but would reflect the potential of heavier, noisier vehicles to create noise nuisance.

4. TRAFFIC MANAGEMENT

Overall urban traffic management

Traffic management systems are used throughout the OECD to achieve a number of complementary objectives which include reducing congestion, reducing both air and noise pollution from vehicles and improving the appearance of town centres. These schemes may be comprehensive in approach, such as the Zurich scheme (Inset 5), and include public sector investment in mass transport systems, improved traffic flows, re–routing of heavy traffic, reduced speed limits, pedestrianisation of inner cities, lorry bans and campaigns to improve driver behaviour.

In several countries, such as the Netherlands, the desire to reduce traffic levels by 20 per cent has led the government to study means of discouraging private and commercial road transport and providing incentives to use public transport. The policy will aim to provide out–of–town parking at stations for high speed train links to city centres, and may introduce some form of road–pricing, despite anticipated technical difficulties.

In Sweden, policy centres on improving public transport and introducing a road charge of SKr 25 (US$4) for every private car trip into the city centre of Stockholm; this is expected to cut emissions of NOx and noise by up to 30 per cent.

More often schemes incorporate only a few of these elements and may apply only to single streets or main thoroughfares. The most common traffic restraint measures include:

— Speed limits (such as those for lorries in Switzerland);
— Narrowing carriageways and introducing artificial bends (often combined with planting, seats and parking, used in some German cities);
— Bans on heavy vehicle movements at sensitive times (in France at weekends, in Germany on Sundays, although this is more aimed at reducing congestion, and in Switzerland at night–time and weekends);

- Restrictions on lorry movements where alternative routes are available (French "quiet town" schemes are an example. In Austria, through–traffic between Germany and Italy may eventually be required to use high–speed rail links);
- Out–of–town lorry parks and freight distribution centres (as at Groningen, in the Netherlands, where operators, including the Post Office, are restricted from the city centre).

In Germany, experiments with noise control use a combination of environmental traffic management approaches. Six towns with populations of up to 1.8 million have been selected for studies of the effects of traffic restraint schemes incorporating the following measures: improvements in public transport; provision for cyclists and pedestrians; speed reductions in residential areas; tree planting; and publicity campaigns. In one town, Buxtehude, the scheme cost DM 5 million (US$2.7 million) for 2.7 km^2 of city centre, but has been successful in reducing noise, while improving road safety and the environmental quality, including recreational use of the city's streets.

Further research into the benefits of reducing inner city speed limits to 30 km/h in German cities indicates that, where this is done without interrupting traffic flow (and, therefore, without increasing unnecessary braking, acceleration and use of gears), noise from passing cars may be reduced by up to 6 dB(A) (equivalent to 4 dB(A) ambient noise level reduction). The German experience suggests that steeply progressive fines act as an inducement for complying with speed limits; an excess of 8 km/h is overlooked to give drivers the benefit of the doubt. The limitations on implementing such schemes generally stem from the need for extra manpower to police traffic restraint zones and from drivers' unwillingness to comply with speed limits if their justification is not fully understood.

Time and space restrictions

Since lorries are the main source of noise nuisance at night from engine, brake and "startle" noise, many towns have tried to ban heavy night–time traffic. These bans may be total or only partial.

In Switzerland, a night–time and weekend ban operates on all heavy vehicle movements, effectively reducing noise during sensitive periods; likewise, under the French "quiet town" schemes, lorries have been completely banished from some city centres such as Audincourt. This has been successful in reducing excess noise by 18 per cent (Inset 6). Elsewhere, the legal opportunities for such drastic policies do not exist and local authorities have managed to operate more selective schemes.

Three such schemes were identified in OECD countries; they have applied time and space restrictions to noisy vehicles only and exempted low–noise vehicles from bans:

- A lorry ban in Salzburg, Austria, restricts the movement of all vehicles over 7.5 tonnes between the hours of 22.00 and 05.00, but offers exemptions for conventional vehicles with an accepted need to operate at night and low–noise vehicles which have plaques fitted identifying them as "lärmarmes Kraftfahrzeug" based on the German definition (Inset 4, above).
- In much of Greater London, a ban operates on lorry movements between 21.00–07.00 on weekdays and over much of the weekend. The scheme offers incentives to some freight hauliers who receive exemption plates on the basis that they need to operate,

Inset 5

Integrated environmental traffic management: Zurich, Switzerland

In Zurich, a 15–year plan is being undertaken by the General Planning Office with the aim of reducing air and noise pollution from traffic.

In order to reduce ambient noise levels in the city from 70 to 65 dB(A) by 1994, the plan either needs to reduce traffic by an average of 50 per cent, and up to 90 per cent on certain routes, or develop a co–ordinated approach including the following measures:

— *Rerouting of traffic from residential areas;*
— *Silencing of noisy vehicles;*
— *Noise barriers and facade insulation;*
— *Pedestrian zones;*
— *Speed limits of 30 km/h (this would be equivalent to reductions in traffic of 50–60 per cent as long as traffic remains free–flowing);*
— *Traffic flow systems (traffic lights, etc.) favouring public transport, cyclists and pedestrians over private car owners;*
— *New noise–absorbent road surfaces.*

The plan relies heavily on encouraging a different traffic modal split by means of incentives to use an improved mass transit system of buses, trains and trams or bicycles (the latter being non–polluting), and disincentives to use private cars. The incentive to change commuter habits is intended to be a cheap and rapid public service comparing favourably with private traffic, which moves at walking pace. As in other areas of traffic management in Switzerland, this scheme is based on informal, practical co–ordination of noise and air pollution policy, although these are dealt with by different divisions.

The budget for this scheme, excluding road resurfacing and an accompanying expansion of the public transport sector, is expected to be approximately SF 80 million (US$50 million) to 1994.

are trying to minimise the nuisance they cause by fitting "hush–kits" to their vehicles, are training their drivers to be environmentally conscious and to drive accordingly, and use the least sensitive routes;

— A comprehensive night–time lorry ban with exemptions for low–noise vehicles also operates in German spa towns, of which Bad Reichenhall is the model (Inset 4, above). This scheme has created a high level of awareness within OECD countries and many municipalities appear interested in some sort of environmental management scheme which offers incentives to use low–noise products.

In order for the schemes to be effective a number of conditions are necessary:

— A legal framework which does not conflict with supranational (e.g. EC) legislation, including a definition of low–noise vehicles. This is most easily permitted in the context of German noise abatement law, whereas in France and the Netherlands, it

Inset 6

"Quiet town" schemes: France

Since 1980, "quiet town" schemes have been started in 24 towns, by municipal authorities in co–operation with the French Ministry of the Environment. The total budget has been FF 72.5 million (US$12 million), half of which has been provided by state subsidy. Towns were originally given contracts for three years, whereupon they were eligible for a 50 per cent state subsidy on all noise–related spending. The budgets for individual towns vary considerably, from a few hundred thousand francs (e.g. Caen) to several million (e.g. Nantes).

The towns which won "ville–pilote" contracts, upon application of their municipal authoities, were: Aix–les–Bains, Angers, Audincourt, Besançon, Blois, Bordeaux, Bobigny, Bourg–en–Bresse, Caen, Clermont–Ferrand, Colmar, Lille, Limoges, Menton, Meyzieu, Montluçon, Nancy, Nantes, Rennes, La Rochelle, Saint–Etienne–du–Rouvray, Suresnes, Toulouse, Tours. No new contracts or renewals have been issued in the last two years. The main noise abatement measures adopted in these schemes, which are co–ordinated by municipal authorities, include:

— *Informing the public about noise through brochures, posters, films and audiovisual aids;*
— *Dealing with complaints on noise;*
— *Making provision for noise in urban policy documents and plans, for example by designing "noise maps";*
— *Soundproofing of public buildings such as schools and medical facilities;*
— *Traffic management;*
— *Provision of out–of–town facilities for noisy sports (e.g. circuit for motorcycles outside Toulouse).*

As many of the schemes are still to be completed, there has been little evaluation as yet of the effects on noise levels. Certain public buildings have been made quieter, e.g. the noise level in a school in Besançon was reduced by 10 dB(A) as a result of soundproofing. Similarly, in Audincourt, over a one–year period, there was an 18 per cent reduction in excessive noise (>70 dB(A)) from vehicles at night due to a night–time ban of lorries from the centre. Certain towns, such as Rennes, have been very active on the land–use planning front and have provided landscaped buffer zones 200 metre wide by highways and ring roads. Public awareness of the noise issue does seem to have improved, as is evidenced by the increase in the number of noise–related complaints after information campaigns are begun.

Certain problems have been identified with the "quiet town" schemes:

— *The number of authorities responsible for dealing with noise has risen (e.g. police, gendarmerie, mayor, local government agencies, etc.) and this has led to inefficiency and delays as approval for planning is passed from one body to another;*

Inset 6 *(cont.)*
"Quiet town" schemes: France

— *noise maps and the results of research have not always been used in designing real land use plans; this appears to be due largely to the legal difficulties in changing the planning status of land when no mechanism exists for compensating the owners for lost potential;*
— *public awareness campaigns have not always had the desired effect; e.g. in Toulouse, huge dB(A) meters on display in streets have increased public awareness, but they tend to be regarded as a "noise game" rather than an incentive to be quieter;*
— *since the state subsidy has been suspended due to lack of resources, it is likely that most towns will not continue if they must finance them alone.*

The schemes have been effective where properly funded and where trained personnel are available, as in Lyon and Toulouse, but it seems that three years is too short a period to create a lasting "noise reflex" and it is clear that funding is necessary if the schemes are to continue.

appears that vehicle restrictions are enforceable where there is an alternative route but changes in regulations are needed to permit a selective approach based on noise;
— Clear delineation of the restricted zone and identifiable exempted vehicles;
— A means of policing or enforcing the bans including provision for fines where bans are broken;
— Co–operation from manufacturers and operators.

The experience from the case studies suggests that several further factors contribute to the schemes' effectiveness. In Germany, public awareness of the noise issue is important in helping operators of low–noise lorries to perceive the economic benefits they gain from enhanced public relations; elsewhere the public are expected to be important in enforcing bans. In addition, the administrators of all the schemes have felt hindered by inability to offer financial assistance to cover the incremental capital costs of low–noise vehicles; in Germany, authorities may now offer up to DM 2 000 (US$1 200) as a subsidy. It is expected to be effective in stimulating the use of low–noise vehicles.

Information and education

Information and education to increase public awareness of traffic noise and the potential for abatement have been piecemeal in comparison to other policies. The two principal strategies are:
— Targeted approaches addressing specific issues and particular groups of people;
— Wide–ranging "anti–noise" campaigns addressing a variety of sources of noise.

Quiet driving

In many countries campaigns urge drivers to drive considerately, use gears efficiently and avoid using horns at night. The most successful have been the most targeted campaigns, aimed at fleets of commercial drivers, particularly in Scandinavia, where low–noise driving has also been shown to be compatible with fuel conservation (through better gear use, etc.) and, therefore, conveys economic benefits.

It is difficult to control personal use of vehicles (such as unnecessary running of engines and joy riding), but in Germany, campaigns against "warming–up" car engines in winter appear helpful. Additionally, technical aids to make low–noise driving more automatic are being tested in driving–school cars with the eventual aim of incorporating this in all driver training.

In addition, the Vibration Research Institute (FIGE)[12] has developed an engine–speed regulator which automatically selects the correct engine speed in relation to city driving. It can be externally activated by infra–red sensors and so can control engine speeds and noise peaks in noise–sensitive areas without any effort from drivers.

In Australia, the State Pollution Control Commission for New South Wales prepares leaflets aimed at increasing drivers' awareness of noisy driving and maintenance of their cars.

Labelling

The other targeted approach to noise, labelling to provide standardized noise emission information and raise consumer awareness, has not been used as extensively for vehicles as for other products in OECD countries. In Germany, however, an "environmental quality" symbol, awarded by an independent jury, has been bestowed on buses, lorries and motorised bicycles, with particularly low–noise characteristics; this label is being used by Hercules, a manufacturer of motorised bicycles who has incorporated "low–noise" into the product name of its "Flüster–Mofa" model. In addition, the requirement for low–noise vehicle operators to receive a subsidy in Bad Reichenhall or Berlin is that they advertise noise levels on their vehicle. As a result, leading manufacturers, Magirus Deutz, Daimler–Benz and MAN have started printing noise levels on the front of the cab of quiet lorries and taxis.

In Australia, the ANZEC (Australian and New Zealand Environment Council) has no power, but provide the basis for co–ordination, endorse methods for measuring noise and recommend specifications for labels. If these are taken up by the more populous states, in practice all products will be noise–labelled. The ANZEC recently decided that all trash collection vehicles should be labelled so that local councils could choose low–noise models.

In Japan, the Environmental Agency demonstrates low–noise electric vehicles at the Low Pollution Vehicle Fair during Environment Week.

In the Netherlands, between 1982 and 1984, the Ministry of the Environment tried to introduce a self–imposed noise certificate to be awarded by the Noise Abatement Foundation. This failed, however, for lack of interest from both manufacturers and consumers. In practice labelling cannot work alone, since customers are more interested in price, fuel economy or safety. Either regulations or financial incentives are needed to stimulate the market for low–noise vehicles.

Campaigns

Wide–ranging "anti–noise" campaigns have been attempted to educate the public about the nuisance from traffic noise. In France, this has been centred on the "quiet town" schemes

(Inset 6, above). Informing the public about noise has been a key element of "quiet town" policy, and awareness of the noise issue appears to have improved, as evidenced by an increase in the number of noise–related complaints after campaigns are begun. In Toulouse, however, where huge dB(A) meters on display in the streets have increased public awareness, they appear to be considered as a "noise game" rather than as an incentive to drive more quietly. No new licenses have been granted or renewed and, in the absence of additional state funding, most of the towns concerned have dropped the schemes as too expensive.

5.   CONTROL OF RECEPTOR NOISE

Consideration of the noise factor in planning

At a general level it is widespread practice in OECD countries to take noise impacts into account, and noise assessments are part of the environmental impact assessment required by local authorities for major new road projects, adaptations of existing roads or installations likely to generate heavy traffic loads. Local authorities generally have the power to withhold licenses but in practice only require the developer to try to minimise noise nuisance by siting the road in a particular way or by creating noise barriers or noise–screening banks.

Zoning

The basic requirement for successful zoning and planning is that planning authorities be able to produce maps visualising noise levels around fixed installations and alongside roads and railways for both present and future situations. In addition to noise maps, a model for calculating noise impacts on specific buildings or areas is necessary. This technical know–how is developed to differing degrees in the case study countries. The Netherlands has developed a sophisticated and easy–to–use system available to all local authority planners.

There are two major approaches once this framework is in place, namely:

— Zoning, whereby a zone adjacent to existing and new roads is earmarked (in the Netherlands, the width of this zone varies from 200–600 metre depending on the number of lanes) as an area where extra attention must be given to the planning of new development and the improvement of existing acoustic environment;
— A system for laying down preferred and maximum permissible noise levels for dwellings adjacent to noisy roads and specifying planning requirements for new buildings.

This information may be used to limit building in the future, or as a basis for compensation. The experience of using the noise factor in planning has varied considerably; in Japan and the Netherlands, zoning alongside roads is now required in all major road developments. In Australia and France, the ability of local municipalities to map out and implement noise–related planning measures varies considerably. In Australia, a few municipalities have introduced building consultation requirements. New dwellings are not forbidden next to noisy roads, but the insulation requirements may discourage developers from building in noisy sites[13]. The effectiveness of this disincentive varies between areas depending on how energetically building regulations are implemented at building and completion stages. In France, the complexity of the classifications to be carried out concerning all roads means that many communes have undertaken the mapping but do not make use of the information, partly because restricting planning use is seen as an infringement of property rights.

In Japan, there have been considerable efforts to introduce a green belt adjacent to major roads and wherever the availability of land allows. New four–lane roads will now be flanked with a 10–20 metre strip which includes roadside barriers, green buffer zones and a footpath between roads and residential areas. Since 1986, cities, towns and villages have had access to interest–free loans to purchase land for buffer zones adjacent to major noise sources. In France, some towns, such as Rennes, protect dwellings from ring road noise with wide strips of landscaped terrain. Elsewhere purchasing strips of land has generally been avoided in favour of reflecting noise by constructing non–sensitive buildings as noise barriers adjacent to roads. This is considered as effective in towns with limited development space for siting warehouses and depots.

A major problem has emerged, however, related to the control of highways, which are often under regional rather than national control. This is the case in France and Germany: local authorities have limited finance and often a limited degree of interest in long–term planning around roads.

Alternative routes

In all countries, the planning of town by–passes to direct heavy traffic towards less sensitive areas is a key part of policy, but putting such plans into practice may be a slow process. In Japan, for instance, whereas 630 municipalities were considered to require by–passes in the 1970s, about 350 had been built by the mid–1980s. These were effective in reducing night–time sound levels by an average of 11 dB(A) (and by up to 22 dB(A) in 21 municipalities).

In Germany, almost 80 per cent of the five year Federal road building programme to 1991, or over DM 5 billion (US$2.7 billion), is intended for building by–passes.

The major problems with building more by–passes are that they are expensive and long to complete and that additional measures to alleviate inner city black spots may be required in the interim. In addition, they may either create greater flows of traffic or merely relocate the problem; this experience has been widespread in OECD countries and careful long–term planning is required to maximise the benefits.

Alleviating "black spots"

Although the focus of traffic noise abatement has been on reducing noise at source, there has been increasing interest in means of intercepting noise where it reaches alarm levels (for instance, along urban motorways) or where shortage of space means noise–sensitive buildings cannot be separated from roads. There are three major means of reducing ambient noise:

— Roadside noise barriers;
— Sound insulation of dwellings;
— Improved road–tyre interfaces.

Roadside noise barriers

In many countries, in response to complaints from residents, noise barriers have been used effectively as a means of reflecting noise at particular black spots, e.g. along highways and at busy interchanges on ordinary roads. Increasingly, environmental impact assessments require that barriers be allowed for in the planning stages of new roads.

In Japan, barriers have been widely in use since the 1970s; by the end of 1986, nearly 200 km of expressways and roads were lined with barriers. Experience in Japan suggests that 3 metre noise barriers can reduce noise by up to 10 dB(A). Along German highways and streets, more than 1 200 km of noise barriers had been built by 1988. The average cost was DM 406 per square metre of barrier wall.

In France, the use of barriers has been rather important since legislation appears to encourage a public, rather than private, compensation approach and it is easier to provide money for noise barriers than subsidies to individuals for insulation. In France, 70 km (220 000 square metre) of noise screens were put up in the 15 years from 1972–87 at a cost of between US$75–200 per square metre. In France, sound–reflective banks of earth have also been used as barriers at a cost of US$40–400 per square metre. Both solutions appear to have similar effectiveness; screens of 2–3 metre achieve noise reductions of approximately 10 dB(A). While landscaping measures may prove more expensive than other barriers, they are likely to involve less conflict between noise and visual environmental objectives. In the Netherlands, sound barriers have been used along 180 km of road. In Norway, sound barriers have also been used for 100 km.

Sound insulation

Insulation of frontages (double glazing) is a quick and highly effective method of reducing serious noise impact in dwellings adjacent to major roads and in circumstances where it is not usual to have windows open. The provision for insulation varies between countries where different thresholds of night–time noise act as a trigger for subsidies (Table 4).

Table 4. **Planning noise levels for insulation of dwellings from road noise**

Country	Planning noise level (dB(A) threshold at dwelling frontage)
Japan	65[a]
Australia	50[b]
France	70[c]
Germany	52 and 62[d]
Netherlands	55-60[e]

a) Or more than 60 dB(A) by certain expressways.
b) With windows and doors open to a total of 5 per cent of floor space. Closed windows and doors: 40 dB(A).
c) Outer walls of dwellings.
d) Sound insulation is paid for from levels over 52 dB(A) (night) and 62 dB(A) (day).
e) Temporarily raised by 5 dB(A).
Source: OECD.

In Japan over 31 000 dwellings had been sound insulated by 1986. In France, buildings exposed to over 70 dB(A) are eligible for insulation grants, but financial aid procedures for relocation of residents most disturbed by noise from new roads or for insulation are separate from restrictions on building rights in noisy zones. Financial assistance is in the form of subsidies to builders from the Ministry of Housing. Funds available were relatively small. Since the average cost per dwelling ranges from US$2 000–4 000, the Construction Directorate has recently decided to leave the Highways Directorate to deal with the problem by building noise barriers or insulating facades of dwellings within 200 metre of noisy roads.

In Australia, local councils in some municipalities apply a code for new multiple–occupancy buildings in areas exposed to more than 50 dB(A) noise from roads; the extra cost of insulation (up to 5 per cent of materials costs) is borne by the developer and ultimately the purchaser. Checks are made during and after building construction and where the standards are not met, builders may be required to complete the work afterwards. This is having the effect of encouraging developers to avoid building on noisy sites and to incorporate good acoustic design from the planning stage to minimise extra costs of higher sound insulation.

In the Netherlands, local authorities are obliged to take noise levels into account when granting permission for new dwellings or roads. In 1986 alone the Ministry of Housing spent Gld 3.5 million (US$1.65 million) on insulating some 2 750 new dwellings. This sum rose to Gld 13 million (US$6.15 million) over the period 1987 to 1988 for the insulation of some 4 000 new houses.

The Dutch experience suggests that it is very much cheaper to insulate houses at the initial building stage (average cost US$615) than to insulate existing dwellings (average cost US$1 400–2 800). This is borne out by the Australian experience and has acted as an incentive for builders there to comply promptly with building regulations in noisy zones.

In Germany, the Ministry of Transport has issued guidelines which are being used as a basis for compensation for installing insulation in dwellings affected by newly built federal highways and roads. Sound insulation has so far been provided in nearly 20 towns, but it is not yet certain that the guidelines will become legal requirements.

Tyre/road–surface noise

As the noise emissions from vehicle propulsion factors, such as that of engines, exhausts and brakes, are systematically reduced, other types of noise, such as tyre/road–surface noise become more important. Road surface noise is particularly important from cars at all speeds and from lorries at high speeds and in wet weather. On specific road surfaces, such as paving blocks, grooved cement concrete, chipped bituminous concrete, and French "anti–skid" surfaces, noise becomes even more apparent.

Although there are no regulations or directives in force in any country, many countries appear to be following one of two options:

— Avoiding "noisy" technologies, such as cement;
— Overlaying noisy surfaces with silent ones.

In several OECD countries such as Austria, Belgium, France, Germany and the Netherlands, research is currently under way to develop road surfaces which are quiet, but are able to withstand winter weather and traffic loads, as well as any conventional surface does.

In Germany, the federal government is financing research and development programmes between 1986 and 1992 to test noise reduction potential and durability of "whispering asphalt" and "sound–absorbent multi–layer roadway"[14]. Although no long–term testing has yet been carried out, initial results suggest reductions of 3–4 dB(A) by using "whispering asphalt" and 5–7 dB(A) by using multi–layer road construction. Similar tests in Austria show "whispering asphalt" to be 3 dB(A) quieter than concrete at high speeds. The first experimental motorway section using this surface has shown no deterioration over three years and all new roads are expected to use it.

In response to this search for quieter materials, the cement industry is considering new forms of "quiet" concrete based on increased particle size. In Belgium, a section of the Brussels ring road has been overlaid with drainage asphalt at a cost of US$3–5 per square metre. The effective noise reduction was 7 dB(A), which speed limits and noise barriers had failed to achieve, even though the latter were ten times more costly than the drainage asphalt.

In the Netherlands, research is also being carried out on quieter road surfaces, especially the characteristics of particle size. In the ten years to come, 1 000 km of the existing highway network (a total of 3 000 km) will be resurfaced with "whispering asphalt".

The major constraints on further work concerning the surface/tyre interface include the following:

— The cost of replacing surfaces of existing roads, although this is less of a problem when roads are due for resurfacing anyway;
— The conflict between safety and quietness — skid resistance requires the maximum possible tyre tread and rough road surface;
— Lack of long–term research on the durability of various surfaces in harsh winter conditions.

Chapter 3

RAIL AND AIR NOISE

1. INTRODUCTION

Levels of noise

In some of the case study countries, exposure of population to rail and air transport is considered as a major cause of noise nuisance. In Australia, for instance, air traffic noise is more widely experienced than nuisance from trains, whereas in Japan, where high speed trains are routed through densely populated cities, the noise arising from such express railways also presents serious problems.

Railway noise

The proportion of people in each country who were exposed to more than 55 dB(A) from railway noise in 1980 varied widely (Table 5). In Switzerland, over 36 per cent of people are exposed to at least 55 dB(A) while in the Netherlands, only 1 per cent experience railway noise nuisance. In Japan, noise from superexpress railways has long been considered a problem but, in Europe, this is comparatively recent. Concern is now being voiced throughout Europe about the environmental impact of new high–speed rail routes.

Table 5. **National population exposure to railway noise, Percentage, 1980**
Daytime sound level in L_{eq} dB(A) outdoor (00.06-22.00)

	> 55	> 60	> 65	> 70	> 75
France (1980)	1.2	0.8	0.4	0.2	–
Germany (1985)	–	4.7	1.7	0.5	0.1
Netherlands (1987)	6.0	1.5	0.6	0.3	0.1
Switzerland (1985)	23.4	13.0	5.9	2.5	0.9

Source: OECD Environmental Data Compendium.

Aircraft noise

Aircraft noise is mainly caused by jet engines during landing and take–off and flight procedures during and after these operations. In Japan, over 300 000 people were exposed to at least 67 dB(A) in 1980; of these almost 21 000 were exposed to more than 82 dB(A). In contrast, in both Australia and Switzerland, the numbers exposed were small, some 1 200 each exposed to up to 72 dB(A) in Australia (1983) and 74 dB(A) in Switzerland (1990) (Table 6).

The number of aircraft in operation has risen in all countries and, despite an increasing focus on the noise problem, is likely to continue rising.

Measures for reducing noise

Railway noise

Until now, railway noise has attracted less attention and efforts to reduce noise have concentrated on zoning and adaptations of rail lines and rolling stock. Insulation and noise barriers are used in some countries, to alleviate noise at black spots, but Japan appears to be the only country where an overall approach to the problem is considered necessary.

In France, the Institute of Transport (INRETS) is undertaking research on the response of communities to noise from new superexpress (TGV) railway lines for the southwest and the proposed northern TGV line.

Aircraft noise

The major policies used to reduce aircraft noise include:
— Emission limits for engine noise;
— Variable noise charges as a component of landing fees;
— Traffic management including time and route limitations for noisy aircraft;
— Land use planning;
— Sound insulation of dwellings and installation of barriers (Figure 2).

2. NOISE LEGISLATION

Emission limits for new aircraft

With the exception of Japan, all the case study countries have been implementing noise level limits for aircraft, based on the International Civil Aviation Organisation (ICAO) noise standards (known as "Annex 16"), since the late 1960s. The limit values for individual aircraft during noisy operations (take–off and landing) are specified in terms of Effective Perceived Noise Levels (EPNL) in decibels, and depend on the weight of the aircraft and the number of engines. ICAO regulations measure the maximum noise experienced at three points: take–off, the start of the aircraft's roll, and during landing. Since 1977, aircraft cannot receive a certificate of airworthiness, unless they meet the maximum emission criteria described in ICAO standards for these three reference points.

Figure 2. MEASURES TO REDUCE AIR AND RAIL NOISE POLLUTION

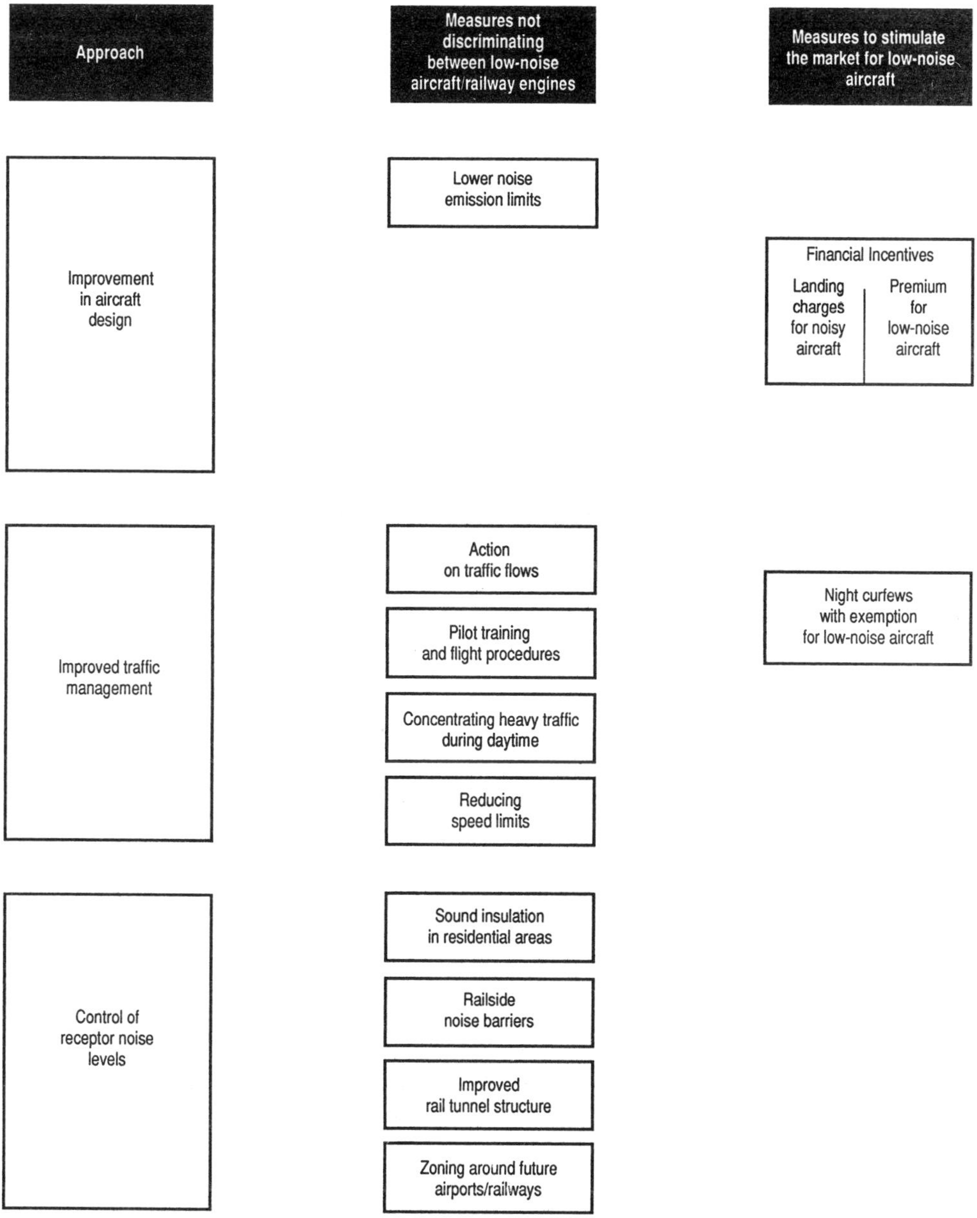

Approach	Measures not discriminating between low-noise aircraft/railway engines	Measures to stimulate the market for low-noise aircraft
Improvement in aircraft design	Lower noise emission limits	Financial Incentives — Landing charges for noisy aircraft / Premium for low-noise aircraft
Improved traffic management	Action on traffic flows; Pilot training and flight procedures; Concentrating heavy traffic during daytime; Reducing speed limits	Night curfews with exemption for low-noise aircraft
Control of receptor noise levels	Sound insulation in residential areas; Railside noise barriers; Improved rail tunnel structure; Zoning around future airports/railways	

Source: OECD.

91

Table 6. **Population living in areas exposed to various noise levels around airports, 1970-1990**

Thousand people exposed to outdoor noise levels expressed in daytime L_{eq}

dB(A)	67	68	72	73	74	75	76	77	80	82
Australia[1]										
1975			2.6							
1985			1.2							
1990			0.7							
Japan[2]										
1980	310.3							177.6		20.8
France										
1975		92.0		38.0				ˀ 2		
Germany										
1981	216.0					10.3				
1990						9.4				
Netherlands										
1977		23.8					6.4			
Switzerland										
1990					1.2					

1. Data refer to L_{eq} (00.07-00.22) values.
2. Data were calculated on the assumption that average household size around airports was 3.3 persons.
Source: OECD Environmental Data Compendium, 1987.

Japan has its own standards under a system called "Certification of conformity to noise standards", made more stringent in 1978.

Noise emission limits do not apply only to jet aircraft; in many countries, limits also exist for propeller–driven aircraft (less than 5.7 tonnes) and helicopters. In Switzerland, it was decided to ban the use of ultra–light aircraft completely to avoid new noise sources.

In all countries, the effect of increasingly tightened regulations has been to encourage airlines to phase out conventional, noisier aircraft and replace them with quieter jet aircraft. At Osaka International Airport in Japan, 180 out of 200 jet flights a day are now made by quieter aircraft; this has considerably reduced noise around the airport. In the Netherlands, 80 per cent of jet aircraft were noise certified by 1986. Since 1987, jets not meeting the regulations may not land or take off within the European Community unless exemption has been granted. The European Community is considering directives which will make it legal for European airports to refuse landing to all aircraft that do not meet ICAO regulations by 2015.

In Australia, neither domestic– nor foreign–operated jet aircraft exceeding 34 tonnes receive licenses if they do not meet ICAO Annex 16 regulations. There are indications that the number of people exposed to severe noise disturbance around Australian airports was reduced by 5–7 per cent between 1980 and 1985 as more stringent regulations were introduced; they were tightened again in 1988. Thus, the regulations appear to be successful in reducing noise disturbance despite increases in traffic.

Noise gains have been achieved by manufacturers quite easily as a by–product of attempts to reduce fuel consumption, but it now seems that a ceiling, so to speak, has been reached and that further reductions will result in additional costs.

Rail regulations

There are no corresponding emission limits for trains since the noise sources are more dispersed and railway noise has not been perceived as such a problem. However, existing regulations in Japan and the Netherlands, and research in France and Denmark are the bases for discussion on what constitute acceptable noise–exposure criteria for nearby dwellings. These could apply internationally and could form the basis of international legislation or regulations.

On the basis of this research[15], suggested acceptable levels have been proposed as follows:

	Daytime	Night–time (if necessary)
Clearly acceptable	60–65 dB(A)	60 dB(A)
Tolerable	70 dB(A)	

The United Kingdom, in particular, is considering what levels to adopt in relation to the high–speed rail link to the Channel Tunnel. In Japan, there has been progress in introducing immission limits and the environmental standards include noise exposure limits for the Shinkansen high–speed railway. In the Netherlands, the maximum permissible noise loads for dwellings near railways are 73 dB(A); the preferred level is 70 dB(A). The German government has recently agreed on limits for railway noise in dwelling areas of 64 dB(A) during daytime and of 54 dB(A) at night. By 2000 these should be reduced to 60 and 57 dB(A) respectively.

In France, on the basis of INRETS research on the TGV "Atlantique" route, guidelines for acceptable noise exposure have been prepared. They are based on the same measurement system as for road traffic[16] and suggest that, since rail traffic noise is generally agreed to be more acceptable than road noise, a level of 65 dB(A) is acceptable in sensitive areas (compared to 60 dB(A) from road traffic). In one state in Australia, maximum levels are set at 60 dB(A)[17], while planning levels are set at 55 dB(A).

Once quality standards have been established, they may be used for zoning and compensation.

3. FINANCIAL INCENTIVES FOR NOISE REDUCTION

Noise charges

Noise–related charges for aircraft were introduced in Japan (1975), Switzerland (1980), the Netherlands (1983) and France (1984). Some 30 European airports now operate some form or another of noise–related charges.

The charges are designed to finance compensation and noise protection for local residents and reflect the noise levels of aircraft. The success of the scheme is dependent on two factors: the level of charges in relation to the overall operating costs of aircraft; and the feasibility of isolating the noise polluters as the payers of charges.

The costs vary between countries. In Japan, in 1983, charges varied between US$100–400 and rose with both noise and weight; the noise charge component made up 28 per cent of landing fees. In Japan, the landing fee is seen to be an effective economic incentive which is consistent with attempts to encourage use of new aircraft to meet air quality improvement goals. In France, the Netherlands and Switzerland, noise charges are in addition to the landing fees. In Switzerland, the maximum tax is US$4.40 a tonne.

In France, the original basis of charges was a levy against passengers rather than airlines; this uniform landing levy was applied from 1973. In 1984, it was turned into a levy on a sliding scale related to noise levels. Clearly the earlier tax offered only indirect incentives to airlines by making them marginally less competitive on some routes. In 1987, a decision by the Conseil d'Etat suppressed the noise charges on the grounds that, in the absence of a specific law, it is illegal to charge a levy without providing a service. In order to reintroduce the charges, a law will be necessary to allow the levying of a parafiscal tax.

In Germany, no charges are made; instead, planes in compliance with ICAO Annex 16 (considered low–noise aircraft) are given reductions in landing fees ranging from 18–22 per cent. At Düsseldorf Airport, airlines using low–noise aircraft are granted a premium. This meant that by 1986, 95.4 per cent of all commercial flights over 20 tonne take–off weight were in compliance with ICAO Annex 16.

The best documented examples of successful noise charges are those in Switzerland (Inset 7).

Compensation

There are no noise charges related to train noise, in any OECD country. However, in Japan the introduction to the general principles concerning railway noise abatement[18] outlines measures which must be taken by the railway companies to control noise at source and to prevent noise damage. These include compensation to schools, hospitals and residents for sound insulation. It could be argued that since noise compensation expenses (for insulation and noise barriers) penalise those responsible for noise and provide redress for those suffering from noise, they are financial incentives to noise abatement. Noise producers, such as airports or railway administrations, know they will be subject to the payment of compensation or may face lengthy litigation.

This approach has been most widely used in existing built–up areas around airports and superexpress railways. Compensation has been used principally to provide insulation as a means of noise abatement.

4. TRAFFIC MANAGEMENT

Aircraft movements

Aircraft noise may also be reduced by air controls such as curfews, landing and take–off restrictions, special procedures, and specification of noise–minimising flight paths. Flight

Inset 7

Aircraft noise charges: Switzerland

Noise fees were introduced at Zurich and Geneva Airports in 1980 as a supplement to landing fees for noisy aircraft. Charges were also introduced at regional airports in 1987 for aircraft up to 5.7 tonnes. The charges are based on five different classes of aircraft, of which only those employing the latest available technology are exempt. These aircraft have emissions at least 5 dB(A) below the certification requirements in ICAO, Annex 16.

Class	Description examples	Charge SF	US$
I	DC8 Series 20–40	400	250
II	Boeing 707 Series 100–400	265	165
III	Boeing 707, BAC 1–11, Boeing 727	200	125
IV	Boeing 737 Series 100/200, 720 B, 727 Series 100/200	135	85
V	Airbus A300, Boeing 737 Series 300, Boeing 747, 757, 767	0	0

Source: Switzerland AIP–FALS–1APP1, 30 September 1988.

This system of charges is supported by a noise monitoring system which has been operating in Zurich since 1965. All flights are now recorded (with information on the flight number, aircraft type and take–off weight) and expected noise levels are compared with actual, measured levels. Each violation of the traffic controllers' recommended procedures prompts a written complaint to the airline, unless valid technical or safety procedures are defined as the cause. A list of all violations is published monthly. Most airlines discipline their pilots on the basis of this information, because it is considered entirely accurate.

As a result of this close co–operation between the airlines and the authorities, only 0.4 per cent of all take–offs, since April 1987, have involved noise violations. The same monitoring system is now being installed at Geneva Airport.

procedures which reduce noise in particularly sensitive areas are used by many airports; they are effective, but involve some costs for operators in terms of longer flight paths and delays. In many countries, there are curfews on night–time flights unless special permits are issued (Table 7).

In Germany and Switzerland, detailed models of noise emissions taking into account flight paths, speeds and procedures plot the optimal mode of operation for each flight. Recommended flight operations often include zooming, cutback zooming and controlling wing flaps — all to reduce engine output noise — and, in congested times, placing holding areas above sparsely populated points.

Table 7. Time restrictions for aircraft operations, at major airports

Country	Time
Australia	23.00-06.00[a]
Germany	23.00-06.00[b]
France	23.00-06.00[c]
Switzerland	24.00-05.00[d]
Netherlands	Night-time
Japan	23.00-06.00

a) Dispensation for low-noise jets.
b) On commercial airports, the restrictions do not apply to low-noise aircraft.
c) At Orly and, for Concorde only, at Charles de Gaulle.
d) 06.00 for take-offs.
Source: OECD.

In Switzerland the airport authorities publish a monthly bulletin for all local communities explaining why permits for night–time landings or take–offs have been allowed, and detailing any changes in traffic density or runway usage. The noise monitoring system is used to reduce aircraft noise emissions at source through pressure brought to bear on individual airlines and pilots (Inset 7). At Schipol Airport, in the Netherlands, an electronic control system has been introduced to enforce the standard instrument procedures.

Sydney Airport in Australia now operates a similar permanent monitoring system which identifies excessive noise from individual aircraft and compiles statistics on aircraft movements and community noise exposure.

In France, if charges are reintroduced in the future, provision could be made so that aircraft not using recommended low–noise flight paths pay an additional levy. An analogous charge on noisy driver behaviour is already used in the German road traffic restraint schemes for drivers contravening "quiet" driving speed limits.

5. RECEPTOR–BASED MEASURES

Land use planning

Most of the case study countries attempt to zone land around major airports. Zones are designed to separate noise–generating and noise–sensitive land uses. This is done by mapping noise contours and relating permissible land uses to ambient noise levels. Noise levels are usually described in relation to two levels: statutory preferred and maximum permissible noise loads for dwellings and noise–sensitive buildings. When a new situation arises (i.e. there is a change in the size or operations of an airport, a new railway is built or new dwellings are built near an airport or railway), noise levels will be used by local authorities for one of two purposes:

— Restricting land use, prohibiting the construction of noise–sensitive buildings in some cases, or insisting on adequate levels of insulation in others;

— Acting as thresholds for compensation for sound insulation or noise barriers.

In the United Kingdom, the Land Compensation Act grants not only compensation in kind, but also compensation for loss of value of property or loss of amenity value. This, however, applies only to residents already living in the area before a certain date. Those moving into the area after airports have been expanded are deemed to have bought houses at discounted prices which reflect noise.

In France, procedures to assist local residents are separate from zoning policies, which designate three zones near airports in which the right to build is restricted but do not incorporate any principle of compensation. Such zoning measures are therefore considered by local communities as an attack on property rights, since loss of development gains, if any, is not compensated. Subsidies to cover costs of installing insulation are provided by housing departments.

Elsewhere, legislation provides allowances for financial compensation or sound insulation (as in Germany, Japan, the Netherlands) (Insets 8, 9 and 10).

In all countries, the noise maps make some attempt to anticipate future developments in terms of traffic growth, flight procedures and changes in runway direction or flight paths in order to restrict building in areas that may experience noise nuisance in the future.

In Japan, where major airports have been built in heavily populated urban areas, attempts are made to orient runways towards the coast and to set aside land as buffer forests and banks in order to reduce the number of flights and flight noise over heavily urbanised areas. This policy is also being followed for zoning along noisy railway lines (Inset 9).

Insulation

Compensation in two forms: soundproofing of property and payment of cash, is often used as a last resort when all other means of noise prevention have been tried. Some countries have adopted special provisions in their legislation allowing for compensation to be granted mainly in kind, for soundproofing of schools, hospitals and dwellings within specified noise contours (France, Germany, Japan, the Netherlands). Only the United Kingdom has established a specific law to compensate landowners for loss of amenity value or for curtailment of property right. The thresholds for compensation differ between countries and the problems associated with using noise maps as a basis for financial payments have sometimes caused difficulties.

In Japan, some 376 000 dwellings had received grants for insulation by the end of 1987; as a result, their indoor sound levels were reduced by between 20–30 dB(A). In Germany, grants of up to DM 130 per square metre (US$70) are available for insulation of dwellings in the highest noise zone (Inset 8) and by the end of 1986 DM 761 million (US$405 million) had been paid out by commercial and defence airfield operators. This was equivalent to 2–2.5 per cent of their operating costs.

In France, between 1973 and 1984, a tax levied by the Airports Authority on all passengers at Paris airports was used to buy up houses most exposed to noise and insulate schools and hospitals. The authorities spent FF 175 million (US$27 million) on house purchases and FF 65 million (US$10 million) on soundproofing; this, however, did not account for all the money collected in taxes due to restrictive provisions on the areas that qualified and only 70 per cent of costs of insulation being eligible for subsidy. In 1984 the tax on passengers was replaced by a noise landing charge on airline operators. The operators challenged the levy, claiming it was illegal because they did not receive a service in exchange. The levy was discontinued. If the charge is to be reintroduced and ear–marked for insulation, it will need to be approved as a parafiscal tax.

Inset 8

Land use planning around airports: Germany

A statutory decree (issued according to the Air Traffic Noise Act, March 1971) divides land around German commercial and military airports into two noise protection areas: Zone I where noise levels exceed 75 dB(A); and Zone II where they exceed 67 dB(A) (1). No residential buildings are permitted in Zone I, while buildings such as hospitals, schools and old people's homes requiring noise protection are not permitted in Zone II. Owners of property in Zone I may claim financial compensation either for structural sound insulation for buildings or for prohibited building activity. A third zone based on a 62 dB(A) limit is also mapped as a voluntary boundary which local authorities can use for long–term planning purposes, given long–term annoyance from aircraft noise and the likelihood of changing flight paths or runway directions in future.

The major problem of the zoning scheme is that it is based not on the current situation, but on the anticipated noise maps in approximately ten years' time, which cannot be drawn up without detailed information on numbers and types of aircraft to be operated, routes and procedures. Despite these difficulties, the noise boundaries must be very precise because of the financial implications for both authorities and residents.

As a result of the introduction of quieter aircraft and improved traffic management, the size of noise protection areas around twenty–four airfields has been reduced.

---

1. On the basis of maximum duration of each flyover for the busiest six months of the year including an extra night flight (22.00–06.00) weighting of 10 dB(A).

Inset 9

Countermeasures against railway noise: Japan

The Shinkansen railway networks have been developed since 1964 as part of a high–speed mass transportation system, but noise from the engine, from brakes and from track vibration have become an increasing problem in urban areas.

In 1974, local residents along the Nagoya railway filed a lawsuit against the National Railway for compensation against noise. In addition to financial compensation, they requested the establishment of a maximum speed limit. Compensation of Y 480 million (US$4 million) was paid and, as a result of negotiations, a decision to attempt to keep average peak levels at 75 dB(A) or less through built up areas was secured.

In March 1976, Environmental Quality Standards (EQS) were laid out in "General Principles for Countermeasures against Shinkansen Railway Noise"[1].

The following standards were to be achieved over a ten–year period between 6 a.m. and midnight.

Zone	Standard value in dB(A)[a] (average peak level)
Mainly residential	70 or less
Commercial and industrial	75 or less

a)   Measurement of 20 successive trains passing either a point considered representative or a point where noise is a problem.

Reductions have been successfully achieved along some 770 km of track at an estimated cost of Y 31.6 billion (US$242 million) through various measures to reduce noise at source. These included placing rubber matting under the tracks, gradually phasing in heavier tracks, polishing corrugated rails, reducing the distance between catenary wires and improving steel girders to reduce vibration, rolling noise and spark noise. In addition, structural changes such as tunnel buffers (acoustic hoods at the mouth of tunnels) have been installed to deflect noise. These reductions have been successful in reducing noise to target levels in many places but when black spots continue to exist, receptor policies have been used instead. These include noise barriers, compensation and land use planning.

Compensation has been paid in the form of insulation for housing. Compensation is payable where noise is above 75 dB(A) for residential dwellings or 70 dB(A) for schools and hospitals. So far 41 000 dwellings have been insulated with effective reductions of 20–30 dB(A) in indoor noise. Sound barriers have also been widely used and are installed for most sections of these two lines. Noise reduction measured from 25 metre away is between 7 and 8 dB(A).

1.   Environmental Quality Standards for Shinkansen Superexpress Railway Noise, Environmental Agency Notification no. 46, 29 June 1975 in accordance with provisions of Article 9 of the Basic Law for Environmental Pollution Control (Law no. 132 of 1967).

Inset 9 *(cont.)*

Countermeasures against railway noise: Japan

Furthermore, in some cases, railway premises and buffer sites are transferred to local authorities so that they may create green belt sites. City plans may also site in such a way as to prevent dwellings clustering along railways.

This combination of policy measures has been effective in reducing railway noise and meeting Environmental Quality Standards in many areas. However, work still needs to be done in some black spots, e.g. along the Tokaido, Sanyo, and Tohaku Joetsu Shinkansen lines where 45 000 dwellings still require insulation.

Inset 10

Land use planning: zones along railways in the Netherlands

In the Netherlands, a government decree which took effect in early 1987[1] makes it possible to establish noise zones of "preferred" and maximum sound levels along railways in "new" situations; either when new tracks are laid, old ones are modified or new houses are built near railways.

Zones of varying width (from 100–500 metre) on either side of tracks are established with the aim that noise outside these zones should not exceed a preferred level of 70 dB(A) or a maximum level of 73 dB(A). The maximum level will be reduced to the current preferred level by 2000; the preferred level will be reduced by a further 3 dB(A).

Overview of planned expenditures on railway noise,
million Gld

	Implemented			Planned		
	1986	1987	1988	1989	1990	1991
Prevention	1.5	0.5	0.5	0.5	0.5	0.5
Improvement through:						
— Barriers and embankments	3.0	3.0	3.0	3.0	3.0	3.0
— Wall insulation	6.4	4.5	4.5	4.5	4.5	4.5
Total	10.9	8.0	8.0	8.0	8.0	8.0

1. Decree on Railway Noise, Government Gazette 1985, 250.
Source: Multi–Year Noise Abatement Programme 1987–91.

Of this expenditure the majority, some 56 per cent, will be on wall insulation, 38 per cent on noise screens and embankments and the remainder on prevention and transition situations by avoiding planning permission for dwellings near noisy railways. A commercially available computer programme has been developed which allows anyone to calculate the noise emission levels to the nearest metre along any track. This is expected to be of considerable assistance to local authorities as a planning tool because it will be easy to assess sound levels for specific buildings and the optimum means of noise abatement.

Chapter 4

DOMESTIC, NEIGHBOURHOOD AND INDUSTRIAL NOISE

1. SOURCES OF NOISE

The various types of noises dealt with in this section may arise from fixed installations, such as factories or construction sites, or from movable sources in mainly residential areas, such as domestic appliances, dogs and recreational noise (e.g. gardening equipment, stereos), and car alarms.

Most national or local planning regulations cover noise emissions from fixed installations such as factories or construction sites and try to reduce noise at source either through encouraging the use of quieter plant and equipment, or through zoning to separate industrial land uses from sensitive residential areas. As in the case of other fixed installations (such as airports, roads and railways) where these policies fail to achieve the required reductions, then insulation or severe restriction of operating times may be used as last resorts.

Since the noise of every day life comes from multiple sources and is often the result of carelessness or ignorance at both national and local levels, it has proved difficult in all of the case study countries to implement effective measures dealing with it. Several policies have been used, with varying degrees of success:

— Ambient noise limits and local ordinances on noise emissions from restaurants, bars and swimming pools. This is usually achieved through joint action by police and environmental agencies at a local rather than national level;
— Restrictions on hours of use of noisy items, particularly domestic appliances and noisy equipment in residential areas;
— Labelling to promote use of lower–noise home appliances and other equipment in residential areas;
— Improved sound insulation;
— Efforts to educate the public to awareness of the noise problem.

2. REGULATORY APPROACHES

Industrial noise regulations

For industrial installations in general, legislation on external noise focuses not on emissions of noise from sources, such as particular machines, but on ambient (immission) levels which are set to protect the public against annoyance. The noise of a particular machine is not considered important to the external environment if there is no population close by, whereas in densely populated areas, relatively quiet equipment may be considered a nuisance. Estimated emission limits for specific pieces of machinery are used in Germany as a guide for land use planning. Plants may be required to meet certain limits in order to qualify for a license.

Industrial noise inside factories or on construction sites, where it involves the exposure of workers to noise nuisance in the course of their work, is usually covered under health and safety legislation rather than environmental regulations. In the Europen Community, there is a legal limit, 90 dB(A), over which employers must provide workers with ear protectors. However, these are not popular with workers and it is considered more important to reduce noise at source by adapting and gradually replacing noisy machinery. The EC legislation also requires regular hearing tests for workers exposed to noise in excess of the limits, thus making it easier for workers to seek compensation for hearing damaged on the job. Where factories decide to reduce noise of machines at source, this will positively affect the external noise environment.

More commonly, external noise from individual sources will be regulated in terms of ambient noise levels in sensitive buildings, such as schools, hospitals and dwellings. In Japan, there have been efforts to tackle neighbourhood noise at several levels through limiting industrial and commercial noise in residential areas. The Noise Regulation Law requires that new facilities submit plans to show that they meet the most recent requirements. In addition, existing factories (such as paper, printing, flour and textile mills) or machines (moulding and metal fabrication machinery, air compressors and earth moving equipment) must not exceed maximum noise limits (Figure 3).

In Germany, the authorities consider the use of state–of–the–art noise abatement technology as a very effective measure to reduce noise from both new and established industrial enterprises. For each country, limits vary between day– and night–time, take account of the level, duration and obtrusiveness of the noise, and define detailed means of measurement. In Japan, in cases where the installation of noise abatement equipment is too costly, particularly for small enterprises, the Small Business Finance Corporation meets removal costs and subsidised buildings are available in industrial sites.

Noise immission standards are generally divided into two categories: maximum permissible limits used for financial compensation, and "preferred" limits, used for land use planning. These may be based on absolute limits or require comparison with background levels. In Switzerland, there is a third category: "alarm" levels between 5–15 dB(A) above maximum levels, used as indicators that these spots require urgent improvement. The range of noise thresholds in selected countries can usefully be compared (Table 8).

Domestic noise regulations

In the case of domestic noise, it has proved difficult to legislate. In most of the case study countries, control of neighbourhood noise depends on local ordinances or police regulations; these are based on the concept of nuisance resulting in complaints rather than on absolute limits. Efforts generally focus on arbitration, use restrictions and education, rather than on enforcing limits through penalties. However, in some states of Australia, where noises are considered "unreasonable" or "offensive", a noise control notice or direction may be served requiring that noise be reduced by a certain date. If this is not achieved, then fines may be applied or court action taken. Only rarely has such action been found necessary.

In the Netherlands, charges levied on noisy installations finance a zoning system around industrial areas (Inset 11).

Figure 3. **MEASURES TO REDUCE DOMESTIC, NEIGHBOURHOOD AND INDUSTRIAL NOISE**

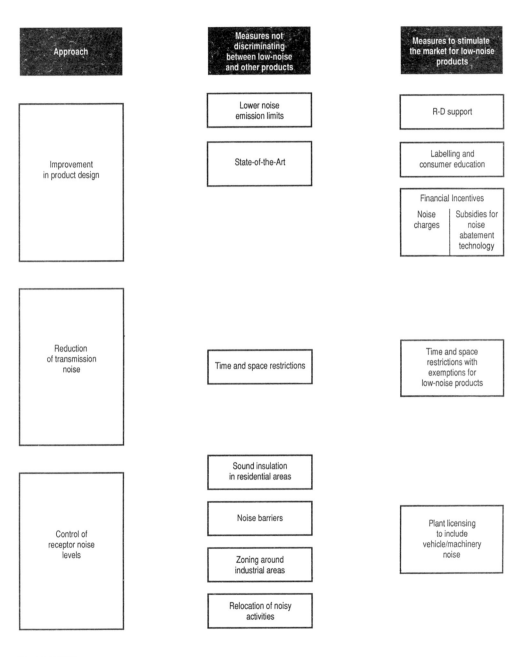

Source: OECD.

Table 8. **Maximum permissible noise loads for industrial noise (dB(A))**

Type of Zone	Australia Night-time[1]	Switzerland Night-time[2]	Germany Night-time[3]	Japan Night-time[4]	Netherlands
Noise sensitive (schools and old people's homes)	30	45	35	40-45	55[5]
Mainly residential	35	50	40	30-50	60[6]
Mixed commercial and residential	40	–	45	50-55	–
Commercial and industrial	50	55	50	–	65[6]
Mainly industrial but some residential	55	60	70	55-65	–

1. Guidelines based on Australian Standard, AS 1055 - 1984. Description and measurement of environmental noise.
2. Impact threshold, recommended limits 5 dB(A) less.
3. Rating level = recommended limit.
4. Noise levels are measured at the factory or site boundary where the machine is in use.
5. New dwellings to be built.
6. Existing dwellings.
Source: OECD.

3. TIME AND SPACE RESTRICTIONS

Industrial operational limits

In Germany, time restrictions on operations may be imposed on plants which do not meet noise standards laid down in the Federal Immission Control Act[19]. Immission limits cover traffic noise from vehicles within the plant boundary, which is often the major cause of night–time noise. Where noise comes from machinery or construction equipment, the regulations require that "state–of–the–art" noise abatement measures be used to minimise emissions. Where noise levels still exceed recommended values, loud machinery may be restricted at night or completely shut down.

If the noise noted during night–time operations is a result of vehicle movements, the authorities may request the use of low–noise vehicles[20]. This is easiest where the enterprise owns its own fleet of vehicles. On the other hand, many premises, particularly retail organisations, receive early morning deliveries from other fleets of vehicles over which they have no control; or noise arises from operational patterns (use of noisy fork–lifts, uncovered loading bays, air brakes) or careless driver behaviour. In extreme cases, the planning authorities may introduce temporary business limitations or recommend that plants be rebuilt further from sensitive areas.

Inset 11

Zoning and industrial noise charges: the Netherlands

In the Netherlands, the Noise Abatement Act, Chapter 5 gives municipal authorities powers to consider the noise issue in dealing with both the allocation of land for new industrial purposes and existing industrial premises.

By September 1986, all municipalities were obliged to establish noise zones around existing industrial areas which cause significant noise nuisance; the intention was to have some 700 zones by mid–1989. The zone should be sufficiently large for the noise levels[1] outside the zone to be 50 dB(A) and maximum permissible levels of existing dwellings within the zone to be 65 dB(A).

The zone should then be used for land use planning; the preferred external noise for new dwellings in the zone is 55 dB(A); if existing or planned dwellings experience higher noise levels, then the local authority must notify the provincial director, who designs an improvement programme. Approximately 500 industrial areas are included in improvement programmes affecting some 72 000 dwellings. The programme aims to reduce noise loads to preferred levels (55 dB(A)) for all dwellings within the next 10 years.

Noise–related charges were introduced for fixed installations in the Netherlands in 1982[2] until 1988. The charge had two specific aims; to raise financial resources for noise abatement and have a deterrent effect on noise polluters. Initially, the charge was levied on the basis of authorised immission levels; it has since been changed into a fuel levy, similar to the road traffic levy.

Before the fuel levy was introduced in 1988, it was estimated that of 1 100 individual plants covered by the Noise Abatement Act, some 80 per cent were paying up to US$10 000 each in noise charges.

In 1987, the programme brought in to some US$11 million, which is spent principally on improvement operations but also on administration at municipal and provincial level and research.

The entire improvement programme is estimated to have a budget of US$275 million over ten years, of which 25 per cent comes from the government as damage indemnification to companies to subsidise measures they cannot finance themselves; the remainder comes from the polluting firms.

In due course noise zoning will be integrated with other environmental objectives involving risk and odour, as has been done at the DSM chemical plant in Limburg.

---

1. Twenty–four hour Leq dB(A) based on daytime noise with added weight of 5 dB(A) for early evening and 10 dB(A) for night–time noise.
2. Industrial noise levies, 1982–83.

Residential areas

In several countries regulations specify permissible hours of operation for various items in residential areas such as sound amplifying equipment, lawn–mowers, power equipment and domestic appliances. The regulations usually state those times of day or night during which such items should not be used if they are audible to neighbours.

In some states of Australia, the use of certain items (e.g. air conditioners, power tools, sound amplifying equipment and lawn–mowers) is prohibited at night if they can be heard from a neighbour's property. Enforcement usually occurs in response to a complaint by neighbours; if the offender fails to stop making noise after having been warned by local council officers or police, a fine of the order of A$250 to A$500 can be applied. In Switzerland, the use of washing machines, lawn–mowers and other household appliances is restricted late in the evening and on weekends. In neither Australia nor Germany may lawn–mowers be used at night–time. In Germany, however, low–noise lawn–mowers may be used until 22.00.

In Japan, in cases where small and medium–sized enterprises cannot afford the necessary noise abatement equipment, they may be encouraged to move to a less noise–sensitive environment.

4. LABELLING

Labelling which provides standardized information on product noise emission levels has attracted interest in OECD countries as an inexpensive means of creating a market for low–noise products. The aim is to increase consumer awareness so that consumers will choose products on the basis of their "quietness" and so create a stimulus for manufacturers to research and develop low–noise products to meet consumer demand. There are four main prerequisites for labelling successful:

— A legal obligation to provide noise labels;
— An easily identifiable label;
— A standardized system of acoustic verification;
— Awareness on the part of consumers.

There has been some experience of noise labelling of lawn–mowers throughout the European Community (Inset 12) and of construction equipment power tools and consumer durables in Germany. Lawn–mower labelling has been achieved but according to manufacturers has had limited effectiveness in forcing development of quieter designs because the accompanying regulations have not been sufficiently stringent. Australia has made the most progress in labelling of equipment used in residential areas (Inset 13), but even there, noise labelling appears to be used only when required by state regulations rather than as a consumer selling point in its own right.

In Switzerland, the Federal Environment Protection Act empowers the authorities to require manufacturers to show noise labels for equipment, but this has not yet been enforced. In Japan, the Environment Agency is considering use of a labelling scheme for "environmental–protection" machines which would include low–noise construction equipment.

5. SOUNDPROOFING

Against external noise

Soundproofing for dwellings is the ultimate method of reducing receptor noise, as opposed to abating neighbourhood and industrial noise at source. This is widespread policy in Japan and the Netherlands wherever noise immissions from new installations or new constructions exceed maximum permissible limits.

Neighbour/internal noise

In both Japan and the Netherlands, zoning and noise maps serve as a basis for compensating dwellings for facade insulation. In the Netherlands, policy focuses on raising awareness in the building and design sector so as to provide improved insulation for new buildings against external as well as internal noise. In Switzerland, the Swiss Society of Engineers and Architects (AIA – Rule 181) lays down mandatory requirements for internal insulation against staircase, heating, ventilation and lift noise and also has stringent requirements for acoustic insulation in zones where noise immissions exceed the limits (Table 8, above).

In France, acoustic insulation has been found to be more effectively used when planned in co–ordination with heat insulation programmes.

6. PUBLIC INFORMATION AND EDUCATION

Authorities in Australia, France, Japan and Switzerland are trying to promote the concept of "quiet" communities with reduced levels of industrial, traffic and domestic noise.

Since 1981, all French chief regional towns have had noise officers, whose job it is to co–ordinate the action of various departments. In Essonnes, the noise officers deal with over

Inset 12

Noise emission limits: the European Community

Since 1984, the European Community has produced a series of directives setting mandatory or guideline noise emission levels and test procedures for construction equipment, lawn–mowers and domestic appliances. The experience in both applying the directives and effectively reducing noise levels varies considerably by product range.

a) *Construction equipment*

Directives were published in 1984 for all equipment, except excavators, which were not covered until 1986. The directives set two–stage noise level goals, the first to be achieved in 18 months and the second in five years. The main provisions were as follows:

— *Type approval testing was to be carried out in a recognised test centre which would issue a noise certificate;*
— *A label with the sound pressure level must be affixed to each product;*
— *Products could be marketed only if they met the noise limits;*
— *Members could take measures to regulate the use of equipment in areas they consider sensitive or in geographically defined areas.*

All Member States appear to have applied the directives, and the appropriate engine modifications have been made in products now marketed. As for the labelling procedures, some manufacturers use the maximum permissible levels and others use the actual test result levels, adding several dB(A) to take account of production tolerances. Some manufacturers expressed the view that labels sometimes reflected test results, but that production models did not actually conform to these limits. Several engine manufacturers in the United Kingdom have started using quiet engines as a marketing criterion but there is not yet any evidence that this is seen as a buying criterion by consumers. Before tighter limits are introduced, clarification is needed of test procedures, particularly for concrete breakers, and test centres must be approved for all countries.

b) *Lawn–mowers*

Directives for lawn–mowers were introduced in 1984 and subsequently amended in 1988. The former directive has been extensively implemented but the 1988 directive is not due to become mandatory until July 1991. The only technical problems reported were for cylinder mowers, for which a compromise has been achieved by fitting a regulator. The provisions are broadly similar to those for construction equipment, with the exception of certification; types are tested but manufacturers provide their own certification and affix labels with the maximum sound levels that they guarantee.

Inset 12 *(cont.)*

Noise emission limits: the European Community

As with construction equipment, no product that meets the limits can be denied entry into any market, but manufacturers can go further and indeed appear to consider low noise a potential selling point. The directive permits individual countries to introduce further limits in areas considered sensitive.

c) *Household appliances*

The directives in relation to household appliances were introduced in 1986 (86/594/EEC) and were due for implementation by the end of 1989. The provisions were not mandatory and may be summarised as follows:

— *Member States may require the publication of information on airborne sound levels of certain appliances;*
— *Guideline conditions for measurement and noise levels are provided if Member States choose to apply them;*
— *Where this is not the case, manufacturers may still label their products according to these guidelines;*
— *This information should be incorporated into other required labels where applicable.*

There is very little evidence of countries incorporating this directive into national law or of manufacturers using labelling. The major barrier appears to be the lack of agreement on any test method.

500 complaints a year, principally concerning pets, domestic noise and appliances (burglar alarms, heating systems, etc.). Although a large number of complaints over aircraft or road noise are also received, the noise officer has no jurisdiction over them and can be successful only if problems are settled amicably.

In some countries, small campaigns (in Switzerland, for instance, the image of a black cat on wheels has been used to promote quiet driving) and slogans (such as "Be neighbourly, it feels nice" or "Quiet Day" in Australia) have been relatively successful, but local experts suggest that only sustained long–term campaigns are successful in increasing awareness of the roles of central agencies and the potential for reducing noise nuisance. In Japan, the experience with raising awareness suggests that poster and pamphlet campaigns are successful only when supported by regulations and economic incentives, for then "quiet communities" are expected to incorporate a range of measures. In France, the experience of the "quiet towns" suggests that sustained programmes are more successful than short–term (three–year) efforts to create noise awareness in town dwellers (Inset 5, above).

In Japan and Switzerland, sustained programmes at municipal level have been successful and are being used as models for noise abatement at a national level (Insets 14 and 15).

Inset 13

Labelling: Australia

The Environmental Noise Control Committee representing the Australian and New Zealand Environment Council (ANZEC) has developed the technical basis for measuring and labelling noise emissions for certain types of equipment, such as lawn–mowers, power tools and domestic appliances, used in residential areas. This is considered as an effective means of tackling neighbourhood noise because it allows states to introduce legislation based on standard methods of measurement. States which wish to encourage low–noise products may legislate that where equipment does not meet specified standards, it is not saleable. Equipment is required to display a noise label.

In New South Wales, the legislation on lawn–mowers has been in effect since 1982, and noise limits have been progressively lowered. Some Australian sources view labelling in conjunction with regulations on permissible noise as "design forcing"; the two prerequisites are that realistic noise goals be set and that the market size justify the research and development costs incurred by manufacturers. In the case of lawn–mowers these conditions have been met and manufacturers have co–operated. In 1979, the average noise of a lawn–mower measured at 7.5 metre was 83 dB(A); by 1987, this had dropped to 70 dB(A) as a result of the introduction of new technology encouraged by a combination of regulations and labelling.

The policy has been less successful in relation to chainsaws, air compressors and pavement breakers, for two reasons. First, since most equipment is imported and since Australia accounts for only 2 per cent of the world market, it has proved difficult to force design changes; second, while initial reductions were easily achieved, it was found that subsequent limits were too low for high–powered chainsaws. As a consequence, policies have been revised and limits of 85 dB(A) for chainsaws will apply in residential areas.

The ANZEC has recommended voluntary limits for air compressors and pavement breakers of 70 and 101 dB(A), respectively. Manufacturers are required to label products for informative purposes only. The use of items with lower than particular noise levels can be specified in particular situations, such as residential areas. Air compressors can be made sufficiently low–noise to meet these recommended standards but at an estimated cost increase of 20 per cent; this means that the units with lower noise levels are being purchased only when their use is required in order to meet regulations in residential areas.

Three states have introduced noise labels for air conditioning in the last three years; a label giving the sound power level of each unit must be affixed but no noise emission limits are in force. As yet, no campaign to educate consumers and advertise the advantages of low–noise products has been undertaken and consumers still appear to

Inset 13 *(cont.)*
Labelling: Australia

buy principally on the basis of cost, although developers and architects are attaching more importance to noise levels in designing new dwellings. There are major two problems in achieving noise reductions: first, many units are imported and the testing and labelling of models is relatively expensive; and second, manufacturers who do comply with regulations fear that, in the absence of enforcement and monitoring, other companies may mislabel products and avoid the costs of reducing noise.

Inset 14

Education and community policing: Switzerland

The "Antibruit" Brigade of the Lausanne police department and the Noise Abatement Group of the Zurich police department have some 25 years of experience in dealing with neighbourhood noise complaints arising from a variety of sources. The Lausanne unit had an annual budget of US$630 000 in 1987 and dealt with 7 556 cases of neighbourhood noise in the following categories:

	% of cases, 1987
Traffic noise (faulty vehicles, bad driving)	73.0
Noise from public activities (restaurants, bars, etc.)	3.6
Industrial noise (equipment, night deliveries, etc.)	0.4
Residential noise (appliances, etc.)	22.6
Construction noise (building machines)	0.4

The number of cases handled doubled between 1977 and 1987; over that period traffic noise, which accounted for nearly three–quarters of all nuisance, had become relatively more important, while all other noise sources, particularly construction, declined as machines became progressively quieter. Noise from radio, television, entertainment and commerce in residential areas remained the second largest focus of anti–noise activity. The assistance may consist of reducing or eliminating the source of noise or helping residents understand unavoidable noise emissions. Because of its success in Lausanne and Geneva, this experiment is being repeated in all major Swiss cities.

Inset 15
Neighbourhood noise: "quiet communities", Japan

In Japan the "Noise Regulation Law" provides for local authorities to take control of local business noise through their own ordinances; by 1988, some 31 prefectures had introduced ordinances for noise control of late night restaurants and bars which are considered a major source of noise nuisance. In particular, 44 prefectures had made efforts to reduce noise from nightclubs after midnight[1] by imposing emission limits or restricting hours of operation. In addition, by–laws have been widely introduced to regulate the time and volume of commercial broadcasting through loudspeakers which have become major sources of noise nuisance. Both sets of by–laws have resulted in considerable reductions in the number of grievances reported.

The Environmental Agency is also promoting a project to create "Quiet Communities" which will be free from neighbourhood noise. Pilot model areas have been chosen in Sapporo, Nagoya and other large cities where neighbourhood noise from businesses, domestic sources and appliances is monitored and analysed. The agency has prepared and distributed leaflets to heighten public awareness of the problems. Residents are then encouraged to participate in discussions to design rules for noise abatement in the neighbourhood. Based on these pilot schemes, a model noise abatement plan is expected to emerge and be applied nationwide to create a network of "Quiet Communities".

Chapter 5

FINAL REMARKS

Despite the introduction of a variety of measures to reduce noise pollution in OECD countries, levels of total noise nuisance from vehicles have not decreased significantly because of the increasing number of vehicles on the road. The growth in traffic is an increasing problem for policy–makers, who will have to introduce a range of noise abatement policies even to maintain the status quo, let alone meet their long term targets for reductions in noise nuisance.

With regard to all of the noise sources considered in this report, there are three possible approaches:

— Limiting noise at source;
— Limiting transmission of noise;
— Reducing noise at receptor level.

Within each of these general policy approaches, a variety of policy actions may be used comprehensively or in isolation. This report focuses on policies which have the potential for international application and are not reliant on specific legal frameworks which are non–transferable to other countries.

Limiting noise at source

This is the largest group of policy actions and includes traditional centralised environmental measures such as standards, regulations and licenses as well as economic incentive measures.

Lower noise emission standards. These may apply to either movable or fixed installations. Few countries have emission limits for fixed installations; the guidelines for particular machines used in German plants are an exception. **Immission standards**, or permissible noise loads, in zones surrounding fixed installations are, however, becoming more widespread, particularly for industrial noise and construction sites. In some cases, there are different standards for a given category of installation depending on the land use of the surrounding area. Noise maps generated by this approach are often used as thresholds for receptor–based policies, such as noise barriers and insulation.

By contrast, emission standards for vehicles, aircraft, construction equipment and domestic appliances are either well–established or in the process of introduction. If emission standards are to be effective in reducing noise at source, they must take account of both technical and economic feasibility. Legislation concentrates on new product models because of the difficulties involved in establishing systems of acoustic verification or in in checking noise emissions once the product is in use.

Testing products in used.   Most regulations deal only with new products, testing them at prototype stage, but testing in–service vehicles in Australia and Japan has been effective in reducing noise from old models during the transition period when new low–noise designs gradually replace old, noisy models.

Research and Development.   Many R&D programmes are carried out as joint ventures between manufacturers, government and operators. Most research has focused on reduction at source of noise from vehicles, equipment and aircraft by modifying engines and layouts, producing low–noise prototypes and testing them in operation. Research is also directed to receptor policies including noise barriers, road and tyre modification, house insulation and opportunities for changing the general public's behaviour (quiet communities, low–noise driving, etc.).

Financial incentives.   These may work in one of two ways: **subsidies** to encourage noise abatement by covering the incremental capital costs of low–noise or noise abatement products or providing operator advantages; **charges** on noise emissions or noisy products which provide operators with an incentive to change to quieter products/technologies and may be used to cross–finance subsidies. The OECD countries have had more experience with subsidies than with charges, except for aircraft noise charges. In order to be successful, subsidies or charges should stimulate manufacturers and operators to go beyond existing regulations by adopting low–noise products/technologies and creating a self–sustaining market. Thus far, success appears to have been limited by two factors: the high cost and open–endedness of schemes when no real tightening of legislation is envisaged in the near future.

Charges have proved difficult to put into effect solely on the basis of noise because of technical difficulties in measuring and controlling many vehicles or pieces of equipment; in practice, therefore, economic disincentives, such as limitations on the place or time of operation have been more widely used (e.g. concerning chainsaws in Australia, or noisy vehicles in Switzerland).

Labelling and consumer education.   These are attracting increasing attention as a means of making information on noise available to consumers and of creating a market for low–noise products as well as popular support and pressure for integrated noise abatement programmes. Although some labelling being introduced on an EC–wide basis for construction equipment and lawn–mowers, most activity is at a municipal or state level. Policies must be long–term in nature in order to arouse consumer awareness, without which noise will become neither a purchasing criterion nor the focus of group action.

Reduction of transmission noise

Environmental traffic management.   It is used in all countries to some extent, either in the form of a comprehensive transport planning policy to encourage the use of public transport and bicycles or in the form of individual targeted actions for specific problems. Actions concerning vehicles and aircraft may include speed limits, rerouting and moderation of traffic flows, but are seldom conceived with the sole objective of noise reduction, although this is often a major benefit. Schemes require careful planning and co–ordination between multiple responsible bodies and considerable resources both for infrastructure and policing.

Driver/pilot training and the behaviour concept.   These have been used effectively to improve aircraft flight procedures and, in rare cases, with regard to commercial vehicle drivers and private motorists; schemes are generally more effective where some incentive is involved, such as fines or official warnings for aircraft operators or fuel savings for commercial vehicles.

Promoting mass transport systems. This aims at reducing the total number of sources of noise, especially vehicles, rather than introducing quieter products; in some cases, public transport is subsidised (e.g. Switzerland), in others, private transport would bear additional taxes (e.g. plans in the Netherlands and in Sweden) to provide economic incentives to change the modal split of traffic. In other cases, the traffic flow of public transport using low–noise vehicles may be improved (faster services in the Netherlands), while private vehicles are impeded by deliberately narrow roads, speed limits and restraint zones (e.g. Germany). In order to be effective, such measures require popular political pressure and a large–scale commitment of resources.

Product bans with exemptions for low–noise products. They are used for vehicles, aircraft and construction products. In Australia, low–noise jets have dispensation from night–time curfews, while in Austria, Germany and the United Kingdom, night–time lorry bans do not apply to low–noise vehicles. Experience of bans with exemptions is more limited in other areas, but some examples do exist. Germany includes vehicle movements as well as machines in noise limits for industrial plants and may not permit night–time operation without noise abatement measures, such as using low–noise vehicles; one state in Australia permits only low–noise chainsaws to be used in residential areas.

Control of receptor noise levels

Land–use planning or zoning. Taking into account noise emissions, this is used in most countries to avoid future conflicts between noise–sensitive buildings and noise–generating installations such as airports, railways, roads and industrial plants. Legislation is based on long–term quality objectives usually establishing two noise thresholds: a maximum permissible level is used as a criterion for other receptor–based policies such as noise barriers and insulation while a preferred noise level is used as the basis for future planning. New buildings can be established in zones exceeding these levels only if future emissions are taken into consideration; either an insulation is provided or there is adequate suitable space for developments. Where there is no framework for offering compensation for loss of development potential, local authorities may find it difficult to resist development pressure.

Noise barriers and new road surfaces. The use of new or existing buildings as acoustic screening for noise–sensitive buildings by roads, railways and industrial sites has been adopted in France and Japan, which have also been extensive users of roadside barriers to deflect traffic noise. Barriers may be effective with regard to train and road noise, but are not for aircraft noise. In addition, they are relatively costly and conflict with visual environmental objectives. Structural changes (to track and bridges) and road surfaces may be equally effective in reducing noise and, in the case of road resurfacing, may be considerably cheaper.

Insulation. It is often provided as compensation in the vicinity of roads, railways or airports for residents exposed to maximum permissible noise levels. In most countries, this is not provided for all dwellings experiencing traffic noise nuisance, but only in black spots where other measures have failed, and where dwellings existed before the noise situation became critical. When new dwellings require insulation, compensation is seldom available, except in the Netherlands, where compensation is paid by the government rather than by the noise polluter (such as the highway, airport or railway authority). Insulation is much cheaper when included in initial building design, and, in most countries, it is necessary to raise the awareness of developers and architects. Insulation is effective as a last resort, but if all dwellings exposed to traffic noise annoyance were insulated, the cost would be enormous.

NOTES AND REFERENCES

1. The "A" weighted sound pressure level is designed to correspond to the subjective intensity of noise to the human ear and is almost universally adopted for the measurement of transport noise. Measurements are given in units of dB(A). Leq is a widely used measure of noise nuisance which averages out varying sound levels over time to an equivalent continuous sound level. The measure is open to criticism on the grounds that occasional noisy events are de–emphasized.

2. OECD (1986), "Fighting Noise", Paris.

3. "Fighting Noise", op. cit.

4. As described in the Road Traffic Licensing Ordinance, Annex XXI, Part 49, Section 3, November 1984.

5. The definition has now been changed to allow only "super–quiet" vehicles with emissions of under 79 dB(A) to qualify for grants (Inset 3).

6. In Luxembourg the government offered subsidies to cover the incremental capital costs for cars with catalytic converters to meet changes in regulations over a two year period. The scheme was not taken up until the last moment because appropriate models were unavailable.

7. Based on interviews with manufacturers, ERL "Incentives for Low–Noise Products", June 1988.

8. Virages, 1981–88, aimed at reducing noise levels to 80 dB(A) amongst other, non–noise objectives.

9. MITI, 1974–78, US$2.5 million loan to reduce noise levels for heavy vehicles and urban buses to 86 dB(A).

10. CAB (or Voertuigtechniek) is an association of sixteen public transport companies in the Netherlands, of which nine provide public transport and seven provide regional services.

11. Circular order 21/4/86 Ministries of Finance, Environment and Energy, Hesse.

12. Forschungsinstitut Gerausche und Erschütteringen.

13. The Australian standard AS 3661 – 1989, Road Traffic Noise Intrusion — Building Siting and Construction, gives guidance for appropriate types of constructions for various road traffic noise exposures. The recommendations are not yet mandatory.

14. Schallabsorbierende mehrschichtige Trasse (SAMT).

15. Walker, J.G., "A Criterion for Acceptability of Railway Noise", Internoise 88, September 1988.

16. Leq (8–20 hours) rather than 24 hours.

17. Leq (24 hours).

18. General Plan for Countermeasures against Shinkansen Railway Noise, 1976.

19. Section 1, para. 5, No. 1, 1974.

20. Annex XXI, Part 49, Section 3, Road Traffic Licensing Ordinance, November 1984.

WHERE TO OBTAIN OECD PUBLICATIONS – OÙ OBTENIR LES PUBLICATIONS DE L'OCDE

Argentina – Argentine
Carlos Hirsch S.R.L.
Galería Güemes, Florida 165, 4° Piso
1333 Buenos Aires   Tel. 30.7122, 331.1787 y 331.2391
Telegram: Hirsch–Baires
Telex: 21112 UAPE–AR. Ref. s/2901
Telefax:(1)331–1787

Australia – Australie
D.A. Book (Aust.) Pty. Ltd.
648 Whitehorse Road, P.O.B 163
Mitcham, Victoria 3132   Tel. (03)873.4411
Telex: AA37911 DA BOOK
Telefax: (03)873.5679

Austria – Autriche
OECD Publications and Information Centre
Schedestrasse 7
5300 Bonn 1 (Germany)   Tel. (0228)21.60.45
Telefax: (0228)26.11.04

Gerold & Co.
Graben 31
Wien I   Tel. (0222)533.50.14

Belgium – Belgique
Jean De Lannoy
Avenue du Roi 202
B–1060 Bruxelles   Tel. (02)538.51.69/538.08.41
Télex: 63220   Telefax: (02) 538.08.41

Canada
Renouf Publishing Company Ltd.
1294 Algoma Road
Ottawa, ON K1B 3W8   Tel. (613)741.4333
Telex: 053–4783   Telefax: (613)741.5439
Stores:
61 Sparks Street
Ottawa, ON K1P 5R1   Tel. (613)238.8985
211 Yonge Street
Toronto, ON M5B 1M4   Tel. (416)363.3171

Federal Publications
165 University Avenue
Toronto, ON M5H 3B8   Tel. (416)581.1552
Telefax: (416)581.1743

Les Publications Fédérales
1185 rue de l'Université
Montréal, PQ H3B 3A7   Tel.(514)954–1633

Les Éditions La Liberté Inc.
3020 Chemin Sainte–Foy
Sainte–Foy, PQ G1X 3V6   Tel. (418)658.3763
Telefax: (418)658.3763

Denmark – Danemark
Munksgaard Export and Subscription Service
35, Norre Sogade, P.O. Box 2148
DK–1016 Kobenhavn K   Tel. (45 33)12.85.70
Telex: 19431 MUNKS DK   Telefax: (45 33)12.93.87

Finland – Finlande
Akateeminen Kirjakauppa
Keskuskatu 1, P.O. Box 128
00100 Helsinki   Tel. (358 0)12141
Telex: 125080   Telefax: (358 0)121.4441

France
OECD/OCDE
Mail Orders/Commandes par correspondance:
2 rue André–Pascal
75775 Paris Cedex 16   Tel. (1)45.24.82.00
Bookshop/Librairie:
33, rue Octave–Feuillet
75016 Paris   Tel. (1)45.24.81.67
        (1)45.24.81.81
Telex: 620 160 OCDE
Telefax: (33–1)45.24.85.00

Librairie de l'Université
12a, rue Nazareth
13090 Aix–en–Provence   Tel. 42.26.18.08

Germany – Allemagne
OECD Publications and Information Centre
Schedestrasse 7
5300 Bonn 1   Tel. (0228)21.60.45
Telefax: (0228)26.11.04

Greece – Grèce
Librairie Kauffmann
28 rue du Stade
105 64 Athens   Tel. 322.21.60
Telex: 218187 LIKA Gr

Hong Kong
Swindon Book Co. Ltd.
13 – 15 Lock Road
Kowloon, Hongkong   Tel. 366 80 31
Telex: 50 441 SWIN HX
Telefax: 739 49 75

Iceland – Islande
Mál Mog Menning
Laugavegi 18, Pósthólf 392
121 Reykjavik   Tel. 15199/24240

India – Inde
Oxford Book and Stationery Co.
Scindia House
New Delhi 110001   Tel. 331.5896/5308
Telex: 31 61990 AM IN
Telefax: (11)332.5993
17 Park Street
Calcutta 700016   Tel. 240832

Indonesia – Indonésie
Pdii–Lipi
P.O. Box 269/JKSMG/88
Jakarta 12790   Tel. 583467
Telex: 62 875

Ireland – Irlande
TDC Publishers – Library Suppliers
12 North Frederick Street
Dublin 1   Tel. 744835/749677
Telex: 33530 TDCP EI Telefax : 748416

Italy – Italie
Libreria Commissionaria Sansoni
Via Benedetto Fortini, 120/10
Casella Post. 552
50125 Firenze   Tel. (055)645415
Telex: 570466   Telefax: (39.55)641257
Via Bartolini 29
20155 Milano   Tel. 365083
La diffusione delle pubblicazioni OCSE viene assicurata dalle
principali librerie ed anche da:
Editrice e Libreria Herder
Piazza Montecitorio 120
00186 Roma   Tel. 679.4628
Telex: NATEL I 621427
Libreria Hoepli
Via Hoepli 5
20121 Milano   Tel. 865446
Telex: 31.33.95 Telefax: (39.2)805.2886
Libreria Scientifica
Dott. Lucio de Biasio "Aeiou"
Via Meravigli 16
20123 Milano   Tel. 807679
Telefax: 800175

Japan– Japon
OECD Publications and Information Centre
Landic Akasaka Building
2–3–4 Akasaka, Minato–ku
Tokyo 107   Tel. (81.3)3586.2016
Telefax: (81.3)3584.7929

Korea – Corée
Kyobo Book Centre Co. Ltd.
P.O. Box 1658, Kwang Hwa Moon
Seoul   Tel. (REP)730.78.91
Telefax: 735.0030

Malaysia/Singapore – Malaisie/Singapour
Co-operative Bookshop Ltd.
University of Malaya
P.O. Box 1127, Jalan Pantai Baru
59700 Kuala Lumpur
Malaysia   Tel. 756.5000/756.5425
Telefax: 757.3661
Information Publications Pte. Ltd.
Pei–Fu Industrial Building
24 New Industrial Road No. 02–06
Singapore 1953   Tel. 283.1786/283.1798
Telefax: 284.8875

Netherlands – Pays–Bas
SDU Uitgeverij
Christoffel Plantijnstraat 2
Postbus 20014
2500 EA's–Gravenhage   Tel. (070 3)78.99.11
Voor bestellingen: Tel. (070 3)78.98.80
Telex: 32486 stdru   Telefax: (070 3)47.63.51

New Zealand – Nouvelle–Zélande
Government Printing Office
Customer Services
33 The Esplanade – P.O. Box 38–900
Petone, Wellington
Tel. (04) 685–555   Telefax: (04)685–333

Norway – Norvège
Narvesen Info Center – NIC
Bertrand Narvesens vei 2
P.O. Box 6125 Etterstad
0602 Oslo 6   Tel. (02)57.33.00
Telex: 79668 NIC N   Telefax: (02)68.19.01

Pakistan
Mirza Book Agency
65 Shahrah Quaid–E–Azam
Lahore 3   Tel. 66839
Telex: 44886 UBL PK. Attn: MIRZA BK

Portugal
Livraria Portugal
Rua do Carmo 70–74
Apart. 2681
1117 Lisboa Codex   Tel. 347.49.82/3/4/5
Telefax: 37 02 64

Singapore/Malaysia – Singapour/Malaisie
See "Malaysia/Singapore – "Voir "Malaisie/Singapour"

Spain – Espagne
Mundi–Prensa Libros S.A.
Castelló 37, Apartado 1223
Madrid 28001   Tel. (91) 431.33.99
Telex: 49370 MPLI   Telefax: 575 39 98
Libreria Internacional AEDOS
Consejo de Ciento 391
08009 –Barcelona   Tel. (93) 301–86–15
Telefax: (93) 317–01–41

Sweden – Suède
Fritzes Fackboksföretaget
Box 16356, S 103 27 STH
Regeringsgatan 12
DS Stockholm   Tel. (08)23.89.00
Telex: 12387 Telefax: (08)20.50.21
Subscription Agency/Abonnements:
Wennergren–Williams AB
Nordenflychtsvagen 74
Box 30004
104 25 Stockholm   Tel. (08)13.67.00
Telex: 19937 Telefax: (08)618.62.36

Switzerland – Suisse
OECD Publications and Information Centre
Schedestrasse 7
5300 Bonn 1 (Germany)   Tel. (0228)21.60.45
Telefax: (0228)26.11.04
Librairie Payot
6 rue Grenus
1211 Genève 11   Tel. (022)731.89.50
Telex: 28356
Subscription Agency – Service des Abonnements
4 place Pépinet – BP 3312
1002 Lausanne   Tel. (021)341.33.31
Telefax: (021)341.33.45
Maditec S.A.
Ch. des Palettes 4
1020 Renens/Lausanne   Tel. (021)635.08.65
Telefax: (021)635.07.80
United Nations Bookshop/Librairie des Nations–Unies
Palais des Nations
1211 Genève 10   Tel. (022)734.60.11 (ext. 48.72)
Telex: 289696 (Attn: Sales)
Telefax: (022)733.98.79

Taiwan – Formose
Good Faith Worldwide Int'l. Co. Ltd.
9th Floor, No. 118, Sec. 2
Chung Hsiao E. Road
Taipei   Tel. 391.7396/391.7397
Telefax: (02) 394.9176

Thailand – Thaïlande
Suksit Siam Co. Ltd.
1715 Rama IV Road, Samyan
Bangkok 5   Tel. 251.1630

Turkey – Turquie
Kültur Yayinlari Is–Türk Ltd. Sti.
Atatürk Bulvari No. 191/Kat. 21
Kavaklidere/Ankara   Tel. 25.07.60
Dolmabahce Cad. No. 29
Besiktas/Istanbul   Tel. 160.71.88
Telex: 43482B

United Kingdom – Royaume–Uni
HMSO
Gen. enquiries   Tel. (071) 873 0011
Postal orders only:
P.O. Box 276, London SW8 5DT
Personal Callers HMSO Bookshop
49 High Holborn, London WC1V 6HB
Telex: 297138 Telefax: 071 873 8463
Branches at: Belfast, Birmingham, Bristol, Edinburgh,
Manchester

United States – États–Unis
OECD Publications and Information Centre
2001 L Street N.W., Suite 700
Washington, D.C. 20036–4095   Tel. (202)785.6323
Telefax: (202)785.0350

Venezuela
Libreria del Este
Avda F. Miranda 52, Aptdo. 60337
Edificio Galipán
Caracas 106   Tel. 951.1705/951.2307/951.1297
Telegram: Libreste Caracas

Yugoslavia – Yougoslavie
Jugoslovenska Knjiga
Knez Mihajlova 2, P.O. Box 36
Beograd   Tel. (011)621.992
Telex: 12466 jk bgd   Telefax: (011)625.970

Orders and inquiries from countries where Distributors have
not yet been appointed should be sent to: OECD Publications
Service, 2 rue André–Pascal, 75775 Paris Cedex 16, France.
Les commandes provenant de pays où l'OCDE n'a pas encore
désigné de distributeur devraient être adressées à : OCDE,
Service des Publications, 2, rue André–Pascal, 75775 Paris
Cedex 16, France.

12/90

OECD PUBLICATIONS, 2 rue André-Pascal, 75775 PARIS CEDEX 16
PRINTED IN FRANCE
(97 91 02 1) ISBN 92-64-13457-3 - No. 45419 1991